The Sound of Cherry Blossoms

THE
SOUND
OF
CHERRY
BLOSSOMS

Zen Lessons
from the Garden
on Contemplative
Design

MARTIN
HAKUBAI MOSKO
& ALXE NODEN

SHAMBHALA BOULDER 2018

Shambhala Publications, Inc.
4720 Walnut Street
Boulder, Colorado 80301
www.shambhala.com

9 8 7 6 5 4 3 2 1

First Edition
Printed in the United States of America

♾ This edition is printed on acid-free paper that meets the American National Standards Institute z39.48 Standard.
♻ This book is printed on 30% postconsumer recycled paper. For more information please visit www.shambhala.com.

Distributed in the United States by Penguin Random House LLC and in Canada by Random House of Canada Ltd

Designed by Lora Zorian

Library of Congress Cataloging-in-Publication Data
Names: Mosko, Martin Hakubai, author. | Noden, Alxe, author.
Title: The sound of cherry blossoms: Zen lessons from the garden on contemplative design / Martin Mosko and Alxe Noden.
Description: First edition. | Boulder: Shambhala, 2018.
Identifiers: LCCN 2017019280 | ISBN 9781611804539 (pbk.: alk. paper)
Subjects: LCSH: Gardens—Design. | Zen Buddhism.
Classification: LCC SB472.45 M57 2018 | DDC 712—dc23
LC record available at https://lccn.loc.gov/2017019280

On the night of the full moon on the sixth of November, on the Garden Island of Kauai, Hawaii, we offer a candle, a flower, and incense to the Buddha: the Ultimate, the Compassionate, and the Wise. May these offerings extend throughout space and time. May this book help its readers to cultivate kindness in heart and vision in life.

CONTENTS

The Process

Opening the Eyes of the Garden

Spaciousness and Not Knowing

THE BEGINNING

In the gap between thoughts, we find freedom and possibility. It's a long way from that first glimpse to full realization, and meanwhile we need a vision of the future so powerful it can pull us out of the morass of our habitual patterns, delusions, insecurities, and distractions. Implementing that vision is the subject of design.

I have been designing, building, and caring for gardens for nearly fifty years. From the beginning, my design work has been joined with my spiritual life and practice. Recognizing this interconnection, I call what I do "contemplative" or "non-dual" design. What does this mean? While I use traditional principles of landscape architecture in my work, I also use methods that create gardens with spirit. This begins with understanding the true nature of what I'm doing: while to some people a garden may be just a space with some plants thrown in, to me a garden is a refuge, a place of reverence. It is a place where spirit meets daily life, and in which there is the possibility of awakening and insight.

I have seen how a garden can affect people's lives in ways both ordinary and profound. A garden potentially has enormous power—not a masculine power of rockets and buildings but a feminine power of beckoning and inviting. It has the power of manifest wisdom. When a garden is able to live up to its true potential, it is the expression of spirit; it is the vital link between Heaven and Earth.

The goal of contemplative design is to establish this vital link. Using

Zen principles, and with the same information and materials as in traditional design, we create transformative environments. Our intention is to bring uplift and lightness to our work, and create an environment where realization is possible. When applied mindfully, these same principles can connect to the spiritual aspects of our lives and allow us to be alive in the present moment.

This book describes my process of contemplative design, from creating the vision for a garden to all the considerations that go into the planning, construction, and maintenance of the space. Here, I don't select plants or plot cookie-cutter landscape designs. Instead, my aim is to present the art and spirit of design.

The work of contemplative design begins with an awareness of our thoughts and feelings, our design goals, and the world around us. To create a true garden, we have to see clearly, without judgment, exactly what is going on in ourselves and the space we are working in. We have to see how our lives are shaped and limited by habitual patterns—both positive and negative—before we can understand how to generate patterns that bring about peace, health, and well-being. When we can work with sincerity, patience, and discipline, we will have the capacity to create a garden (and a life) where we can be fully alive and aware of our connections to one another and our natural environment.

Design work in any field is about intentional living. We repeatedly return to awareness of our thoughts, our feelings, and the processes of our cognition. Only by doing so are we able to see and analyze how our habitual patterns manifest physically, bringing either benefit or harm to our environment, our institutions, our culture, and ourselves. When we understand how to join Heaven and Earth in the garden, we understand how to transform our lives, work, and environment into a field of dynamic balance and harmony. Design is the template. It teaches us how to live a meaningful and happy life and how to integrate our spiritual lives and our daily lives.

The secret to happiness is to unite the spiritual with the ordinary, to join Heaven and Earth. My own path has been to create gardens. I was introduced to the link between spiritual work and gardening in 1965 when I joined the Peace Corps and was sent to India. While there I went to the ashram of Shri Anandamurti (Prabhat Ranjan Sarkar), an Indian philosopher and yogi who initiated me into the practice of basic meditation: sitting with an upright spine and using a mantra as I followed my breath as it flowed in and out. When I breathed in, I listened for the sound "hum" and when I breathed out, I listened for the sound "so." I practiced assiduously on my own when I was back in the small village where I lived. Though the Peace Corps had trained me in poultry husbandry, they emphasized that I should try to find out what the community, which was divided into castes, subcastes, and three religions, wanted to do. In my village, what they wanted was a public park. So there I was, meditating in the morning and the evening and figuring out how to design and build a garden. From that time forward my spiritual life and my work life have evolved together, like a pair of aging hands.

Later, my path was very much influenced by two of my teachers. The first was the venerable Chögyam Trungpa Rinpoche. I met him in 1973 at his center in Vermont. He was a Tibetan teacher, a lama who had given up his monk's robes. When he moved to Boulder in 1974, I followed him. There I went to see him for an interview and asked him if I could be the shrine keeper. He told me no. "Instead," he said, "you should stabilize your living situation and build Japanese-style gardens at an American scale." This has been my practice ever since.

The second teacher who strongly influenced my garden design sensibility was Kobun Roshi, a Japanese Zen teacher. He and Trungpa Rinpoche were close, and I had the good fortune of studying extensively with both of them. Rinpoche was always my teacher, but Kobun was not only my teacher but as close to me as my brother. Kobun ordained me and sent me to Japan to study Zen with his own elder brother, Tenzan Keibun, and to study gardening with a garden master. While in Japan, Keibun ordained me and became my Zen master. It is through him that I inherit the Soto Zen lineage.

What I have learned is that spirit lives in the ordinary stuff of life. We can't look to our teachers and think that their understanding is unattainable for us because we do not live in caves in India or Tibet, or in a monastery. For most of us, we have to find our happiness in the activities of secular life. This is our opportunity. This is also where the subject of design arises—the instant we wake up and realize that how we live is who we are we are on the path of contemplative design. Studying design is both learning and training. It is good in the beginning, good in the middle, and good at the end. This is an enjoyable pursuit. Let us cultivate the field of design.

Though the projects I do professionally are usually large, the principles I use are for every project and every person—homeowners and professional designers alike. While this book explains the full potential of the garden and the process of contemplative garden design, the ideas described here can be applied to any path and by anyone who is trying to bring meaning to their daily lives and vision to their actions. May it be of benefit.

THE VIEW

The wooden man starts to sing, the
stone woman gets up dancing.

—from the "Song of the Precious Mirror Samadhi,"
Soto Zen School of Japan

Before we can design or build anything, we have to examine our goals, our motivation, the poetry we are trying to manifest, the language in which we are going to speak, and the underlying principles of composition. The understanding of all these things together is what I call "the View."

START MINDFULLY AND WITH A CLEAR VISION

My first Sanskrit teacher was eighty-two years old. His age limited him to teaching only one class, and he said that he would teach the beginners, because "if they don't get it right from the beginning, they'll never get it right." Something will always be off, and that intangible flaw will resist solutions applied afterward. The View is the basis of all the rest of what we do. This is important whether you're building a garden, a society, or a business, sitting down to meditate, or teaching a class. Without a guiding view, everything we do is reactive and lacking coherence.

Vision is very much absent in our world today. There is very little vision in education or government or in how we lead our daily lives. We fumble along life's pathways with no idea of where we are going or why. The beginning step in making our lives meaningful is creating and sustaining a vision. This is certainly true of creating a garden.

CLARIFY YOUR DEFINITIONS

We have all been in gardens—even very costly ones—that we find oddly uninspiring. There are the landscapes around mansions where money has been lavished on moving trees, building pools, patios, and fire pits, and planting lush lawns, yet we don't much enjoy being in those spaces and may even find them stale and uncomfortable. People can spend a lot for a deeply unsatisfying garden. And we have all experienced the small dead spaces outside commercial areas like hotels and grocery stores where we wonder why they even bothered with "landscaping."

So what is the difference between these sad landscaped spaces and the gardens I talk about in this book? A garden built on Zen principles joins Heaven and Earth. This kind of garden is where we can find our true selves and where we can completely relax without losing awareness of all that is around us. In fact, the compelling sensory experiences of the garden will magnetize our attention and bring us to the present moment. Once we are awake in the moment, the serenity, harmony, and balance of the garden give us the chance to experience who we really are, to have insight into our true nature.

For me, the garden is a place that allows us access to big mind (that which is open, welcoming, and vulnerable) beyond our small mind (the ego-driven mind that is never satisfied and self-protective), a place that is sacred as it engages us with something beyond ourselves. It is a space in which we can find not only pleasure and ease but also insight and wisdom. The garden reflects the clear and quiet mind from which its design arose.

In order to create a true garden, we have to figure out what we are aiming for. We have to define what the garden is. Successful gardens have certain characteristics that we can see and feel; we should set an intention at the outset to bring these characteristics into our design. If the target we're aiming for is unclear, we have little chance of hitting it. Though we can't control what befalls us, we can certainly clarify what we want from our work and our lives, rather than flailing around helplessly in reaction to circumstances. The same is true for garden design. It's useful to begin your transformation with a clear definition of your goal. When defining a contemplative garden we want to consider the following characteristics.

The Garden Is an Energetic System

A garden is defined by its location, its contents (attributes, behaviors, and relationships), and its boundaries. It is a world in itself, a complete but evolving whole. A garden is more than a way to improve the functionality or the resale value of a home, business, or institution. It has its own structure and composition and a personality that seeks expression, and it is beyond style and concepts. For example, Japanese garden styles are difficult to import to certain areas of the United States, where climate conditions and cultural references are so different. However, the underlying principles of Japanese garden design are accessible and can be employed in other cultures and environments.

The whole of your life is an energy system as well. It contains your family, friends, coworkers, and other people, the environment in which you all live, and the way you all relate to each other and to the environment. Making changes to one part of the system is going to affect the whole and all the rest of the parts.

The Garden Is a Quiet Place at Its Heart

While it may be a place for play and entertainment, a garden will also give us the space to connect with spirit. It is a place where everything is alive and where we come alive. Its quiet nature gives us the space to feel and live more fully. As a result, we feel joined to it. There are benefits to that connection: it can restore our energetic balance and harmony and promote relaxation of mind and body. The garden awakens our soft heart. We have a chance to see who we really are. This is only possible because the garden is peaceful, not a place for agitation or worry. The garden absorbs our attention with its beauty and vivacity, drawing us out of our self-referential state.

The Garden Is a Place That Holds Our Memories and Where We Create Memories

Once a group of priests were planning to visit a new national monument in Oklahoma, the site of an Indian massacre. Before they went, they met with an elder of the Cherokee Nation. The elder told them that they should listen to the river at the site, where the tears of suffering could still be heard. Beside the river was an ancient tree that also remembered the suffering, and the tall grasses nearby cried with the unresolved pain of the past. This elder understood that the landscape feels and remembers. And many who have visited Auschwitz or the various 9/11 memorial sites report feeling echoes of the trauma that occurred in these places.

The same can be true of the more positive memories that are made in a garden. The garden remembers our birthday celebrations, the weddings that took place there, and other happy moments. The garden retains the imprint of those who inhabit it. A well-designed garden can create the kind of calm and spaciousness that encourage insight. The repository of memories is then a force for good in our lives.

The Garden Is a Place That Fosters Connection and Relationships

A friend of ours has had to move frequently to follow her husband on business. Wherever she goes, she digs up her mother's roses and irises and takes them along. Watching them grow and flower again in each new space brings her a sense of home and allows her to connect to the new space. In our own garden we have my mother's cherry trees and my father's roses. Especially when they bloom, I am linked to my home of the past and the beloved ones who occupied it. This sense of connection is an important aspect of what the garden is.

The Garden Promotes Not Just Our Spiritual Health, but Our Physical and Mental Health as Well

A healthy organism is integrated, with every cell and every organ helping and informing the others. One reason a well-integrated organism is a healthy one is that all the parts are connected and available to one another. All channels are open. If there is a challenge to a particular part, all the other parts contribute what they can to help.

When we enter an integrated and alive environment, we immediately sense its underlying order. Our bodies and minds can respond to this and connect to our own health and inborn order.

A great deal of research has been done on the adverse health effects of the physical, chemical, and biological hazards in our environment. But a healthy, calm, orderly environment has been less studied. We go about our lives creating environments all the time—in our homes, our cars, and our cubicles at work. At an unconscious level we all are aware of how mess and disorder can make us feel unhappy and limited. What we don't seem to realize is the degree to which we are creating a feedback loop between our environments and ourselves. Driving in a car strewn with food wrappers or papers is not conducive to calm and focused driving. Experiencing a garden filled with beauty and order will almost certainly allow us to calm and clarify our minds, and it will lift our spirits.

The Garden Is a Place That Offers the Possibility of Realization

When all of our senses are magnetized, we can experience a dropping away of mind and body and a loss of self-centered identification. This gives us the opportunity to step outside our habitual thought patterns. In a sense, our experience of who we are becomes the garden and the garden is at peace with all things. This is a very good environment for understanding something about who we are and why we are here.

In the garden, personal transformation can occur. What we are, who we think we are, and how we present ourselves are accumulations of thoughts, perceptual patterns, actions, and emotions, which get linked together and form our story line, the way we identify ourselves. From our personal story line we generate habits of thought, behavior, posture, and movement. Being in the garden gives us the opportunity to return to the present moment—to the bee's buzz on the flower, the soft breeze—and to interrupt habitual patterns. This interruption is an opportunity for awareness to shine through to the face of unborn consciousness.

The Garden Joins Heaven and Earth

"Heaven" is the mind—but big mind, not ego mind. It is innocent and curious and without self-reference. "Earth" is form, mass, structure: the stuff of our ordinary reality. When the two meet, the inchoate mind infuses the material world with its properties. The intention to wed these two aspects of our experience is the heart of garden design, as it is—or should be—the aspiration of any kind of design or art. When we marry Heaven and Earth, the result is a space of joy, inspiration, elegance, and delight. From the moment we enter it, we can feel we have entered a sacred space. Its peace provides a setting where we can relate to our sorrows, our losses, and our misfortunes, as well as our basic caring for our world and those around us. The sense of uplift and balance provides opportunity for renewal, regeneration, and healing.

This is not an entry into some other realm; it is an awakening to the extraordinary nature of ordinary experience. We are able to touch something that is already in us. Kodo Sawaki Roshi once said that "no matter how long you practice zazen, you'll never become anything special." The garden is not Disney World or some "wow!" moment; it is a place to experience ourselves as we are, in peace, perhaps for the first time.

The garden, which reflects and exhibits not an ideal order but the natural order of consciousness itself, embraces change, growth and decay, birth and death, deep stillness, and the movement of falling water. It exists beyond time in the fragile embrace of impermanence. Since that is also the way we exist, the garden is a reflection of us, and we are a reflection of the garden.

WORK WITH THE ACTIVE FORCES AVAILABLE

Our environment influences us physically, emotionally, and spiritually. It is essential that the designer understand the various ways in which a garden can affect us in order to design spaces that create positive effects. The garden is not merely a passive background for activity; it can also be a force for awakening. It affects us by performing the four following actions:

magnetizing, enriching, pacifying, and destroying. We should understand each of these forces so that we can enhance their effects in the design.

Magnetizing

In the garden all of our senses become fully alive and alert. Sounds, sights, textures, smells, and tastes beckon to us from every direction. They call out for our attention, one after the other, so that we are continuously drawn out of our self-absorption. The dew on the purple petal, the light flickering through the branches of the tree, the reflection of the heron in the sunlight of the pond, all serve to trap our wandering minds and bring them to the present moment. The garden presents us with views and experiences that capture our attention.

Enriching

The sensual feast of the garden is enriching. The display of texture, color, form, smell, sound, and light feeds our senses like a five-course meal does our palate. Contrast and variety awaken our sensitivity and stimulate our awareness. Form and color feed our souls and enrich our sense of being fully alive. The beauty of the garden reveals the inherent elegance of reality and lifts our mood.

Pacifying

The garden pacifies our worries and anxieties. Because it is a safe, coherent space with clear boundaries, it allows us to relax deeply. We are not confronted with conflict and unbalanced relationships. Everything is in a dynamic process of refined integration. The tendency of human consciousness is to meld with its surroundings. Sensory input and consequent perception allow the garden to pacify our conflicting emotions and self-doubt. Disruptive environments pit one force against another; in the garden, everything is integrated and interdependent. Our anger and aggression are transformed.

Destroying

And last, the garden destroys our self-clinging. We are continuously presented with something that engages us and as a result we are unable to hold on to the image we have of ourselves. The garden destroys the continuity of our mental story line by interrupting its flow and bringing us to an awareness of the world that is larger than the ego and to which we are intimately connected.

These forces exist and act upon us whether we are aware of them or not. It makes sense for the designer to use them in a conscious way to enhance their properties and the power of the garden.

UNDERSTAND THE LANGUAGE
YOU HAVE TO WORK WITH

Every subject has its own language. In architecture it includes structure and strength of materials; the design of a grocery store speaks in terms of the flow of customers through the space; interior design requires an understanding of the emotional effects of color and object arrangement; auto mechanics have to understand the language of the movement of air and its meeting with energy to create combustion.

The language of the garden is the language of nature. It includes biology, geology, chemistry, ecology, energy, interrelationships, and process. A designer has to be familiar with this language, just as a lawyer has to be able to read a contract or an accountant has to understand a profit and loss statement. A part of every job is mastering its language.

When we consider the language of the garden, we can choose to go about it with a reactive mind unaware of itself, or we can incorporate a larger vision into the process. We have the opportunity to see the elements we work with in a mundane way or to go beyond that simplistic understanding to see the other dimensions in which the elements exist. We can choose a language that can usefully talk about spiritual vision.

The language of contemplative design uses the grammar of the five elements: earth, water, fire, air, and space. We use these elements as the language to create a poem of a space, one that invites spirit. Rather than talk about drip or spray irrigation or where a fire pit might go, we can talk about the garden using these five elements. This gives us a common vocabulary for design and a means to see how each part relates to the others. I find it useful to use the five elements because it breaks the complexity of the design into easily understood chunks. Even physicists use only a few particles to describe the makeup and behavior of the entire universe. The five elements are not limitations but a language to describe the entire garden mandala.

It's important to understand that the physical manifestations of the elemental energies *are* those energies, not mere representations of them. The dirt and rocks embody the energy of the earth element, for example.

Earth

Earth is the basis of the garden. The earth element is solid and unmoving. It is a quiet presence that is the ground on which all other elements are developed. The earth element is primary. If it is properly designed, the other elements are easily integrated into the landscape. Water, pathways, and planting areas all take their place once the earth has been properly formed.

The earth element is a part of every living system; it is the structural basis for everything. In a business, it is the manner in which physical elements and people are organized. In a body, it is the skeleton and my-ofascial tissue. As we work with earth, we should ensure that the structure we are creating can carry the vision of our organization forward, properly support the other elements, and sustain change.

Water

The water element has no form of its own but assumes the form the earth element defines. It is the passive side of structure. Water is reflective; it was our ancestors' first mirror, the only opportunity to see their own faces. It is the element of purity and cleanliness, and it metaphorically relates to clarity of mind.

There is a lot of similarity between the nature of water and the nature of mind. Both become cloudy with agitation and clear when still and settled. Both are fluid and take the shape of whatever they encounter. They can become polluted through continual misuse and abuse, or clarified through proper filtration. When I look at the water lily paintings of Monet, I see images of the true nature of mind, beyond concept and fabrication. In contemplative design, we must use water's qualities of clarity and transparency.

The water element has no beginning and no end. It changes state from ice to liquid to steam, from ocean to clouds to rain to rivers. The rivers return to the ocean, the steam condenses to liquid, and the liquid freezes, becoming ice. Water is neither created nor destroyed.

Many people ask if it is necessary to express the water element in the garden. If you want to join Heaven and Earth, water is essential. It can be a small water basin if properly situated or a dry waterfall and pond (as in *karesansui* gardens in Japan). Indoors, water can be a fish tank, a fountain, or a window since glass has many qualities of water.

Fire

The fire element is energy. It is heat, combustion, and transformation. In our bodies, fire is what digests our food and gives us energy. The fire of a business is its operation, the energy that moves goods from factory to store to shelves.

In a garden, the fire element can be literally fire itself in the form of a fire pit, a fire ring, or a fireplace fueled by either wood or gas. In contemplative design it is more than literal fire and its qualities. Primal fire, the original fire, is the sun. The sun is both heat and light. In the rainbow we see that the light of the sun is made of seven colors and from these all other colors emerge.

Plants are the manifestation of the sun on the earth. They are the children of Heaven and Earth, and they praise the sun with every color of the rainbow as they flower and bend toward the light.

Air

Air is the flow of design. It uses the same principles as planning the flow of traffic through a city or the progress of shoppers through a store. It is movement. In contemplative design we emphasize slow, mindful walking with quiet places to sit along the way.

The air element is the dimension of movement in the garden, comprising pathways and stopping places. Pathways allow us to move through the garden, physically and visually. Stopping places are where we pause to contemplate a beautiful view, where we can be hidden from sight for privacy, or where we can look back to appreciate the journey we've taken. The stopping place sets the point of view from which the landscape is observed. It is our primary point of reference for creating a balanced and beautiful composition.

Composition is based on how the eye travels, on how we visually move through the garden. We are relentlessly looking for patterns and for similarities. We look for similar shapes and forms, heights, colors, qualities, proportions, and spacing. We sort for scale and contrast and look for patterns there. In the stopping place we want our minds to rest and be quiet and our hearts to open. Often the best aesthetic to create this is one of simplicity and elegance.

Space

The fifth element is space. It is the background, what is left out, the container, the binding element.

The space element is the vision that drives all the other elements. It is the ultimate mystery and source of wonder. Space is difficult to talk about since it is the union of subject and object. It is beyond all dualism. Space penetrates all existence and contains everything with nothing excluded. It is unborn, uncreated. It does not appear or disappear.

The experience of space is shaped with our senses. Visually, space is the play of dark and light. It is also the emptiness between forms that brings clarity to the whole. We can hear space in the song of a distant bird or an echo in an empty room. If we stand at the edge of a cliff, we can sense the empty space in front of us through the uprush of air on our skin.

When we use space in a contemplative design, we might leave something slightly unfinished in order to engage the viewer's imagination. We can leave out an element in the rhythm of plantings—like a gap in a line of trees—in order to surprise the viewer and draw her into the present moment.

In the garden we balance light and shadow and use them to achieve our objectives. This balance is brilliantly handled in historic Italian gardens, like Villa d'Este in Tivoli and the Medici gardens in Florence. It is called "chiaroscuro," the use of light and shadow.

These gardens also demonstrate the use of hedges, trees, sculptures, water, and walkways to change our experience of space—a narrow corridor opens to a wide space, or leads from dark, shadowy areas to light, airy ones. Each change in space changes our emotional reaction to the landscape.

From deep stillness the poetry of place springs forth in dressed-up majesty. Earth, water, fire, air, and space express its natural order.

USE YOUR LANGUAGE TO CREATE POETRY

Before we consider how to approach a particular design, the first questions we should ask are: What is the poetry of this garden? What do we want it to *feel* like? This is often the most challenging part of garden design—we have some inchoate dream of a garden but never describe it to ourselves. We might know the pieces we want but not what the landscape as a whole might be.

A contemplative design goes beyond mere style. Sure, I've had clients ask for a "Zen" garden or a "southwestern" garden, thinking that those terms will somehow result in a garden that matches the one in their imagination. But these words are about style and not about the underlying feeling of the space. A style describes a certain arrangement of materials that can be copied. But the underlying cultural references may not translate well into every environment.

Rather than choosing a garden style, we might consider what we will do in the garden. This question of purpose is deeper than what uses the garden will have; it is a questioning of the underlying assumptions about what a garden really means and what you or the client hope it will do. The designer should ask himself and/or his clients (whether they be individual homeowners, a board of directors, or a community): What are the goals for this project? How will people behave in the space? What will be the nature and quality of their experience? What kind of feeling or feelings do they want the garden to elicit?

One might answer the question of goals by saying, "I want a place for my dogs to run and play, a place for my children to experience nature, a vegetable garden, and a large patio to share with my friends." Yet when we look more deeply, we might find that we are looking for the peace and tranquility we feel sitting by a stream with nothing to do or the joy we feel hearing the birds sing in early spring. I had one client who hesitantly asked me if I could design a garden she had seen in one of her dreams from childhood. These vulnerable moments are hard to express and talk about. Designers have to listen deeply to the client or themselves for the unspoken aspiration, the connection to the imagination.

Once we clarify and can express the garden's intent and poetry, everything else in the design flows naturally. Poetry is shaped by a connected series of parts that include the way the space is formed (topography, pathways, and views), the elements within it (the plants, structures, water, pathways, rock formations), and its entrances and exits. Each of these parts reveals the intent of the garden.

This is part of the View that can't be skipped. It is the basis for the vision of everything that follows. You'll know where to cut when the budget gets tight because you'll understand what is not essential to the poetry of the place. You'll see when elements should be added, what colors will be needed.

———

STUDY THE MANDALA PRINCIPLE

Taken as a whole, the garden—like your life—is a mandala, an integrated energetic space that is complete in itself. A mandala is a bounded system in which none of its parts exist on their own. They are defined by and exist because of a complex set of relationships to the boundary and to the things within it. A rock may have a sense of personality in its bearing, but it still exists in relation to the earth on which it sits, the other rocks, and the environment in which it participates.

Though this is easy to understand, you may find it much more difficult to put into practice. Our dominant worldview is that things exist on their own, independent of conditions and influences, and that we also exist as independent, objective beings. Yet, as President Obama once commented, any claim of being a "self-made man" ignores the conditions, structures, and systems to which the whole society contributed that make personal success possible: the roads used, the education offered, the energy and communication systems, and so on. Each piece was built and maintained by all of us. We are all dependent upon each other for our very lives, yet we desperately cling to the idea that we exist independently, not contingently.

To approach contemplative garden design requires a meditative mind that needs training and constant cultivation. We can't create a mandala of interrelated, interpenetrating, interbeing objects, attributes, behaviors, relationships, flows, and meanings unless we ourselves become part of this same system. We do not exist independently of what we are designing and creating. We are the garden and the garden is us.

We occupy a unique location and have unique mass, form, behaviors, relationships, and so on, but all of these factors exist only because of their place in the mandala. There is no independent existence. There is no you and no me apart from other people and the earth and the wind and the sun. We exist because of numberless causal factors—our genetics, the love of our mothers and fathers, our place in time, the food we eat, the air we breathe, the water we drink, and so on. And we are defined by our relationships to others and to our world. This is the matrix in which we act. When designing a garden we will again and again remind ourselves of this and cultivate the mind that thinks in unfolding, evolving energetic systems. Because a garden is a complete mandala, its parts relate to one another. Together they form one whole energetic system. The parts are inseparable from the whole, and the whole is inseparable from its parts, and both are in process of changing.

We are familiar with more traditional, two-dimensional representations of mandalas, like Tibetan mandala paintings, Native American sand paintings, or round European cathedral windows, and there are even three-dimensional mandalas made by Tibetans and others. These are representations of mandalas, intended as the basis for meditative visualization on the perfect worlds they depict. In contrast, the correctly designed garden is a mandala itself, in which the proper placement of living forms in space offers a place for realization.

UNDERSTAND SCALE AND PROPORTION

As with any art, creating a garden relies on certain underlying principles to orchestrate its elements. I use these design principles in my work, as do many landscape architects, but there is a difference in content, emphasis, and application. The principles have to be congruent with the goals and aspirations of the client and harmonize with the physical, cultural, and spiritual environment.

Scale is a means of determining how you will relate to your environment. Do you want to feel dominating and powerful or small and hidden when in the garden? Whatever the feeling we are aiming for, the entire garden should be carefully calibrated so that all of its parts are in proper scale to the overall vision and to each other.

Scale is relative to the viewer. It is our innate sense of measure. It is both a measure of the angle between the sight line and the object, and a function of distance from the observer. For example, a stone that is six feet high looks large if it is six feet from a sitting person, whose eye level is at about three and a half feet. If that stone were twenty feet away from the same person, the sense of how large it is would be reduced. Its mass also appears much less impressive when it is far away.

Proportion is a mathematical relationship between lines, areas, and volumes. It is like the mix of spices in a recipe that stay in proportion even if we increase the amounts of all ingredients to feed more people (the scale). In the garden, for example, if we have three mounds, and mound A is eight feet high, mound B is five feet high, and mound C is three feet high, the proportional relationship between A and B is 5:8 and between C and A is 3:8.

Since ancient times, people have understood proportion as a basis of beauty. Pythagoras showed that by touching a vibrating string at mathematical intervals, he could create harmonious sound relationships, like the octave. The architects of the Parthenon understood the importance of proportion and scale to create a monumental effect. If you changed the height of its pillars, for example, you'd have a completely different experience of the place.

There is nothing new about these principles, but when utilizing them in the garden, we have to keep in mind that the garden is a living entity, which means continued growth as well as death and change. A tree that works perfectly to suggest the height of a mountain will be less effective as it continues to grow and becomes out of proportion to its surrounding rocks. This is one reason that correct maintenance is critical to the garden. If plants grow too tall (or die off and wilt) in relation to their surroundings, then the original scale and proportions of the design will be lost.

One aspect of playing with scale is to allow the microcosm of the garden to play off the macrocosm of its surroundings. We can accomplish this either by repetition of shapes and/or plants or by deliberately setting a view from the garden into the area beyond. For example, if the garden looks out onto a mountain in the background, a smaller mountain inside the garden will create the illusion that it is a foothill of the larger landscape. It establishes a relationship between the garden mandala and the larger environmental mandala. This is called *shakkei* (borrowed scenery) in Japanese garden design.

Shakkei is an important technique used to heighten awareness and a sense of integration. When we borrow from a distant mountain or tree, a cloud, or a landform outside the garden, and establish a close relationship between it and some composition inside the garden, we link the garden's bounded system to its larger world. From this we can extrapolate an understanding of how systems exist within systems and how they are all interconnected. We move from the sense of constraints to limitlessness, infinity, and timelessness. This allows a shift of perspective from the ephemeral to the eternal and from the small mind to the big mind. It allows us to view our lives and our work from a higher perspective where we see ourselves through the lens of interconnecting relationships, all of which are connected to spirit, the ultimate network.

SEARCH FOR BALANCE AND HARMONY

No matter what time of day or what season we enter the garden, we experience a sense of place and feelings of peace and calm. It's important for a designer to understand what contributes to this and why. Since all of the elements of the garden are in a state of constant change, how can we create an ongoing sense of balance and harmony between them? Our lives are continually in flux as well, so how do we find an internal balance and harmony? The same lessons apply to the garden as to life.

Balance is an internally experienced sense that the elements of the garden or of our lives are in correct relation and proportion to one another to suit our overall vision. We almost all have an innate sense of balance: it is what alerts us when a picture is hanging crookedly on the wall. Like all senses, balance can be learned and refined.

Balance is something the designer aspires to, yet never fully accomplishes. Creating it depends upon a sense of internal balance. The sense of when a garden is balanced can depend to some extent on taste and style. In a desert garden, a huge waterfall and pool system can be wholly out of place, though the same amount of water might be perfect in a lush tropical garden of the same size. I like to use a lot of rock in my designs, maybe more than would be to the taste of others, but I try to make sure that the rock is always in proper balance with the other aspects of the design.

In the same way, we all seek a balance in our lives that works for us individually at the stage of life we are in and for our families and societies. We are aware of the need to balance work and family life, for example, though which takes precedence will continually change with specific circumstances. Still, we should have a clear view of the ideal balance in our minds, in order to work toward it. We should also understand the need to balance silence and quiet with the urge to engage with our families and friends; the need to balance indulgence with discipline; the need to balance compassion with correct action toward someone who is creating disturbance. These are all dynamic situations: as with the garden, things change with time and season, and our ideal balance will change also.

An old friend, now in her nineties, says that she continually searches for new balance in her life. She used to swim laps every day and loved to bake pies and bread. Now she can't do any of those things and is learning to let go of the old vision of how her life should be balanced. Her priorities have changed: she wants to spend more time with friends, tell more stories, and bake less. The key to finding balance is to let go of our attachments to previous situations so that we can adapt to new circumstances. If in the garden we find we have to pull out some plants because they don't harmonize with others or they grow too tall, so too do we have to make adjustments to things in our lives that no longer balance other elements. This might mean moving, leaving a job, or putting more time into helping a teenager through a difficult transition. If we are attached to one way of doing things, the stasis will choke us as the world changes around us.

Within its boundaries the garden is at peace and in harmony with itself and with its environment. It does not exist in isolation but within a larger environment of energetic, physical, emotional, social, cultural, and other systems that are all intimately related. This means that the plants and other materials are not jarringly at odds with their environment. For instance, putting a lush tropical garden in a desert setting will typically feel strange and off-putting.

Harmony is like the sound of a deep, clear, underlying tone. The spirit of the garden is so palpable and true that it is the basis of clear insight. That perfect tone is in tune with reality, the way things actually exist in themselves and in relation to each other. If we could find this perfect tone in our own lives, we could balance all the elements. If we operate from an even, clear base, we have a better chance of finding harmonious relationships with our families, coworkers, clients, friends, and so on.

Maintaining balance and harmony in an ever-changing environment requires that while designing, building, and (most importantly) taking care of the garden, we keep adaptation in mind so that balance and harmony can be adjusted as the dynamics of the garden change. This means that the designer needs to clearly understand the vision and the personality of the garden. This will inform how he encourages some growth, such as strong tree branches, and discourages other growth, such as invasive weeds or dominating bully plants.

Most important in developing a balanced plan for the garden is a clear vision of the garden from the beginning. If we've thoroughly understood the goals of the garden and the qualities of the land on which we are building, we have a good chance of creating a design that has an ongoing coherence.

WALK IN BEAUTY, SEEK IT AND CREATE IT

Is beauty an individual experience so personal that we can't relate to others' understanding of it or make general statements about it? Or is beauty a shared experience, with things we can all agree are beautiful: the moon peeking through a cloud, the spread tail of a peacock, an ancient tree, Michelangelo's *David*? Certainly a dog or a goat, if they experience beauty at all, would experience it differently than a person. If we look at what we call "beauty" can we discover a definition on which we can all agree? As designers we should understand how we perceive and process beauty so that it is evident in our designs. It is in the experience of beauty that we recognize big mind.

One attribute of beauty is an underlying organization that can come from symmetry, poetry, color, and other qualities of materials. Our brains are hardwired to perceive this order, even when it is expressed in a complex visual way. We seek order, and nearly universally, we prefer some kind of organization. For example, if we look at a tree that has never been pruned—with colliding branches, dead wood, suckers rising from the base, and no light or air passing through it—we are not likely to consider it beautiful. But with proper trimming to reveal the tree's inherent health, strength, and structure, the tree will appear beautiful, no matter who is viewing it.

Though we can appreciate underlying structure and coherence, beauty is beyond mathematical ideals and perfect symmetry. A design based on a mathematical model like the golden mean might be wonderful, but it is not necessarily a contemplative design. Even a sensitive organization of all the materials in the space is not enough. The contemplative garden comes from the process of its creation and from the fact that its elements are living nature—these are the added factors that create its beauty.

Another quality of beauty is evanescence. When we see a drop of dew on a petal, its beauty arises in part because we know that in a moment this sight will pass. The garden saturates us with the feeling of transience, the sense that some of the things we see there will never exist again. It is like ice in a pocket, a fleeting thing that we can't hold on to.

Beautiful things, whether momentary or lasting in nature, grab our attention and startle us into the present moment. They can interrupt our internal discourse and compel us to look, to sense, to absorb the things around us. We can connect with the beauty in a garden not just through our sense of sight but through all of our senses—feeling the cool shade of a tree, smelling the damp ground, and hearing the wind through leaves.

The beauty of the garden, or of anything else in our lives, awakens something within us beyond our daily concerns. When we are engaged with beauty, we can opt out of our ordinary distractions. Beauty gives us the possibility of getting away from the small sense of ourselves and to become connected with nature and with the larger world.

With the experience of beauty, one gets a sense of the divine. Here on the island of Kauai, the mountains are extraordinarily beautiful, and they each seem to be inhabited by a divine spirit. The mountains in Anahola have a healing energy, while the hills around Hanalei are the playground of the magic dragon, and those on the Na Pali coast evoke the ancients. Nature gives us the sense that there is something greater than our small selves.

Beauty is not always dependent on material ideas, which include proportion, scale, texture, color, chiaroscuro, and so on. Sometimes a concept is beautiful. A sewage plant may smell awful, but the idea of waste being reprocessed and water cleaned is beautiful. The sewage plant in Vienna was designed by the artist Hundertwasser. There, beautiful concept meets beautiful architecture. The mathematician sees elegant solutions to difficult problems as beautiful. The astronomer sees distant galaxies as beautiful. The biologist sees the life of a cell as a universe of wonder. In all these examples, beauty links us with some divine presence, a field of wonder, and some underlying order to the chaos of our daily lives.

———

FIND MEANING THROUGH INSIGHT, TAKE LESSONS FROM NATURE

Rather than trying to answer the eternal question, Who am I and what am I doing here? with circular, intellectualized concepts all seen from an egocentric point of view, we can enter the garden and release ourselves from this small thinking. When we do this, the opportunity arises to transform insight into meaning. We become involved in the beauty and meaning of the garden's parts and relationships and at ease with its birth, decay, and death. We can see how water runs into a rock and simply goes around it and recognize how we have dealt with our obstacles by being too stubborn and unwilling to yield. If we had followed the lesson of the water, we could have continued along our pathway more easily. A tree, which is deeply rooted and in its verticality reaches to the sky, can inspire an architect to better understand how to join Heaven and Earth in her design of a house.

Designing a garden is like writing music. Stravinsky's *The Rite of Spring* may evoke springtime, but what that means to the listener is very personal and for the most part inexpressible. The same music can bring a person to tears and another to joy. Both have had meaningful experiences of the music. The composer (the designer of sound) provides an auditory environment for meaningful experience but does not try to control that experience.

It is possible to convey specific meanings through the symbols we use. There are gardens to commemorate historical events such as the 9/11 attack. There are gardens organized around a concept such as illustration of a poem. We can use materials and symbols that will convey specific meaning to a group of people that will use a garden, like a Christian cross in a church garden or an eternal flame for a grave memorial.

But when we design a contemplative garden we are not limited to this kind of specialized meaning. We are not trying to use materials to say something that a viewer then understands in the same way we do. Instead, we are creating a space that provides an opportunity for insight through quieting and opening the mind. The designer creates an environment that is integrated. The rocks, the trees, the plants, the water, and the pathways are all interrelated and talk to one another. Little flowers talk to each other and to big plants, and rocks within a grouping chatter away and talk to other families of rocks. It is an environment that seduces the senses and heightens awareness. There is an underlying poetic organization that is expressive and palpable. These and the other principles of garden design provide an environment for realization. Realization is where the meaning of the garden happens.

This is why it's important to create beautiful garden environments in which we can lose ourselves enough to discover insights otherwise hidden by our involvement with busy, unstructured spaces that only encourage distraction. Once there is insight, it's possible to find meaning and direction. If small daily tasks have meaning, it's because they are part of a larger project of seeing ourselves as we actually are, and mindfully connecting our small selves with big mind. Every single activity is rife with possibility for that connection, whether it's washing dishes or writing a memo or brushing our teeth. But if these activities occur in a place that is chaotic and ugly, we're less likely to have the quiet mind needed to make the connections we want.

Meaning is something more than momentary. It is not found in the latest design fashion, such as minimalist, expressionist, or whatever movement is trendy. I've known many designers who follow the latest trends, and whose designs are like collages of the popular. Some become famous and wealthy, but their work goes as quickly as it comes. When we wrote our first book ten years ago, we revisited gardens I had built over a twenty-five- to thirty-year period and were surprised to find that all but one of them were in pristine condition. The owners had added their personalities to the design, but in all cases, this enhanced and broadened the magic of the garden.

TURN ASPIRATIONS INTO PRACTICAL GOALS

The design process is about translating the poetry of the garden into precise elements. Once the desired feeling is articulated, you turn your attention to the practical ways of making that feeling come alive through the materials you have.

While poetry is emotional, the goals of the design are more practical: What exactly will the design accomplish, in order of importance? Once the design goal is determined, that goal, that primary purpose, will inform everything.

The designer's goals and motivations can be quite different from the client's, as long as they include all of the client's aspirations. Very few people ask for a sacred space, although that might be exactly what they really want. Most of us don't know how to look deeply into our motivations and aspirations. We might say we want a first-class irrigation system and a landscape that will add value to the house. When we look deeply, we remember our first memory of being in nature and the magic of that experience. We remember the odors and the tactile sensations of being in that space as a young child. Maybe we were climbing a tree or hiding from our brother under a shrub. There is poignancy to those memories and a longing in their remembrance, and the design will fail if it doesn't connect with these feelings.

From this beginning we'll gradually formulate a vision, a design. We have to be careful not to aim too low. A high vision can contain all of the needs of a lesser vision, but it doesn't work the other way around. If we listen too literally and provide a functional irrigation system, an adequate patio space, a dog run, and a playground, the client might be disappointed, even though we have satisfied quite properly all of their stated goals.

We also listen to our own story line. What is our motivation and how does it align with the project's goals? We need an alignment right at the beginning. Otherwise, the relationship will deteriorate and trust will evaporate. While the goals and motivations of the designer and the client can be different, they need to be aligned and workable.

I find it useful to explicitly state first my aspirations for doing the project to myself. When we are talking about creating a garden, we might think that it should join Heaven, Earth, and Man, be an expression of awakened mind, and/or be a place of transformation, leading to well-being. These goals are not exclusive. They are not in conflict with a dog run, a large patio with an outdoor kitchen, or a place for the children to play. However, they are in conflict with a client whose goals involve unsustainable use of resources, negative impact on the existing landscape, and/or disregard for the environment, the culture, or the history of the place. When the client's motivations and goals cannot be incorporated into the designer's motivations and goals, it is best to step aside in the beginning and avoid the inevitable negative outcome.

EXAMINE AND CORRECT YOUR MOTIVATION

Not only should we understand our goals for the garden, but we should also examine our own motivation as designers. The design is not a product; it is a process of interaction between us and a specific space.

Every project should begin with a careful awareness of motivation. The motivation for making a contemplative garden is to create a space that is uplifting and that offers the possibility of full awakening to all who enter it. It's a lofty goal, and not one that's easy to meet, especially when you're designing for someone disagreeable or with a budget too small for the space, or for what seems like "background" space—parking lots, alley entries, or the like. Yet the motivation should be the same every time we sit down to design.

It is not enough to make something beautiful and functional. It is counterproductive to create landscapes to become famous or to get a better design job in the future or to make money from a wealthy client. It's not suitable to have a client satisfied only by the grandeur or size of the garden. This kind of small-minded thinking invariably leads to designs that lack essential qualities of peace and sacredness. I know from personal experience that when I've undertaken a design for a client who has nothing but his ego in mind, or just in order to keep my staff busy and pay the bills, the garden just doesn't seem right in the end. So this first motion toward design, understanding and clarifying motivation, is critical.

For the creator of a garden, examination of motivation is not only a project-by-project activity, it is a daily requirement. Each morning when we wake up, we ask ourselves what our intentions are for the day. If our motivations are not altruistic, if there is the slightest taint of ego clinging or self-serving in our intentions, there is little hope that our actions will be beneficial. In the evening, we review the day's activities and examine them in the light of our altruistic aspiration. We never reach a point where this becomes unnecessary.

This kind of careful examination of motivation shouldn't be limited to landscape designers; it's a useful exercise for all of us, no matter what our profession. If we can clearly list our highest aspirations, in general and for the day, we can make decisions based on this standard rather than on momentary impulses.

LEARN MEDITATION AS THE FOUNDATION OF CONTEMPLATIVE DESIGN

The garden arises from our creative minds. How do we contact our creative minds? We are absorbed in our habits and conventions, and they fill every moment with thoughts that run in well-worn ruts. We worry about our families, our jobs, our homes. We daydream of great accomplishments that will draw attention to ourselves so that everyone we know will compliment and admire us. We plot out ways to be happier, and we rue the missteps that have brought us misery. With all of this going on, there's not much extra space for a new thought, a new approach to problems.

Yet from those spaces, those gaps in the wall of thought, come creative ideas and different ways of thinking and acting and making things. Without creative thought, our only means of solving our problems or figuring things out is through intellectual analysis or emotional reactions, like greed or desire. We are trapped by old mental processes and can't find a better way to handle things.

The better way, the creative way, requires space, room for ideas to arise amidst the chatter of our busy minds. We can create that space through meditation. Meditation is the key to the entire View; you cannot understand the contemplative garden without it. A lot of people think that meditation is all about transcendence or euphoria or bliss, but that is not at all the point. Meditation enables us to examine our own minds to see how they work and to realize that we are not simply our thoughts or emotions. Thoughts that arise are just that: thoughts. They aren't the essence of who we are, and they don't have to rule our lives.

When we commit to sitting in meditation for a certain period, we don't act on the thoughts that arise during that period. For a half hour or an hour or whatever period we've chosen, we instead watch as our minds follow their usual patterns. If we suddenly think, "Oh, I'd like a piece of chocolate cake," we don't hop up from our seat and seek out chocolate cake. Instead, we see it for what it is—a thought—and do as Suzuki Roshi, a great Zen teacher, suggested: we let it come in the front door of our minds and then let it go out the back door. We don't get attached to that thought or give it credibility or get angry at it or pursue it in a train of thought, we just see it for what it is and let it go. Before the next thought arises there is a gap, a hole, an interruption in the stream of thought, and in those gaps is pure awareness.

The more we can reside in that awareness, the more space we are allowing for creative mind to arise. Freed from our habitual thinking, we can wander off the trail and discover new things about ourselves. Meditation gives us the chance, not (at least at first) to remake ourselves, but to know ourselves and appreciate our unique abilities. We are then able to use those abilities in new ways, in creative ways that we'd never suspected possible. Creativity is exploration and discovery of the unknown, and it is fostered in meditation.

While creativity arises in the gap, the unformulated, unknowable space between thoughts, it takes skill to express the creative notion, and skill comes from practice and repetition. Einstein, for example, saw special relativity appear to him from this unknowable fundament, but it took his training and practice as a mathematician to give it expression.

When these creative ideas come, they want to be expressed in the material world, to take form. In this way the Heaven finds its manifestation in Earth, in the things we can see and hear and feel and touch.

Each step of the design process begins with a return to raw awareness, unfettered mind. Once we experience this limitless mind, we stabilize and cultivate it through meditation. Today there are many good sources to learn how to meditate and cultivate mindfulness, so I won't go into great detail here. However, here are a few key points to observe.

We begin meditation with an altruistic motivation. If we are doing this for self-improvement, such as greater productivity and better health, we might experience some benefit initially, but ultimately our efforts will be undermined by our own self-involvement. The altruistic motivation does not come automatically. We have to look deeply into our lives and understand how many of our thoughts are about anger, desire, and ignorance. The altruistic motivation first applies to our own situation. When we see how we cause others and ourselves so much pain, anxiety, worry, and fear, we realize that to live meaningfully, we need to take control of our own minds. Control doesn't happen through willfulness. First we need to embrace our situation and work from this point of reference; we need to feel compassion for ourselves and others.

It can sometimes be difficult to feel compassion. We might recall the kindness of our mothers or someone who cared for us, changed our diapers, fed us, nurtured us, and loved us. This might open our hearts. We might recall a beloved pet who comforted us with its devotion or a teacher who helped us out. Everyone has some reference to a compassionate heart. Once we contact this soft spot, we need to cultivate and nurture it.

We begin by sitting in a comfortable position. There is misunderstanding generally about what is really comfortable for the human body. We think that if we slouch on a couch that we are comfortable. It is true that some muscles relax in that position, but others are shortened and our breath becomes shallow. We might define the relaxed state as a condition where all the muscles in the body are in an equal state of tension. In other words, there is an even distribution of stress throughout the body. Markers of this condition are a straight back and unrestricted breath.

Begin by sitting in a chair or on the floor with legs crossed or on your knees on a meditation bench. It is important to feel grounded, connected to the earth. So, if you are sitting on a chair, bring awareness to the feet. Feel the space between the floor and the feet. Feel the contact with the floor. If sitting on the floor on a cushion with crossed legs, try to have the knees firmly on the floor. The triangle between the knees and the sit bones makes a stable basis on which to build the posture.

Sit up so that the line between the base of your spine and the top of your head is straight. Allow your body to structure itself along this line. Notice particularly the position of your head and its relation to the shoulders. You may need to draw in your chin to give length to your neck. If your chin is up, the curve in your neck will be exaggerated. It may even crimp the line at that point. Your shoulder blades drop back and down and your chest opens up. Your breath, which habitually may be confined to the upper chest, will drop to the bottom of the diaphragm.

Awareness of posture is the first awareness. Next is awareness of the breath. Bring your attention to your breath. Watch it go in and out. Concentrate fully on the breath. It may help to count the out-breath: one, two, three, and so on up to ten, and then repeat. This gives our monkey mind a simple and clear focus.

With an attitude of caring and gentleness, we make friends with our own minds. We welcome everything and everyone into our meditation, like friends who have come over for a visit. Gradually our awareness becomes more concentrated and panoramic. Conflicting emotions and negativity, once welcomed gracefully into our practice, loosen their grip on our attention. Maybe they don't go away, but a greater sense of space surrounds them.

In the beginning this is difficult. Your busy mind will constantly intrude. It might object to the practice altogether or jump from here to there. This is no problem. Let the mind do what it will, but when you notice that your posture has changed or you are no longer following your breath, straighten up and return to the practice. At first it seems there is no space between thoughts. One begins as soon as the other stops. But if you return to the practice, soon you will notice that there is a small gap between the thoughts, a gap where nothing is happening. It is in that gap we learn to reside and find our true home. This is called "the practice of nonthinking." The senses become intensified. You might hear the sound of your circulatory system and your nervous system as two high-pitched internal hums. You might notice the shadow flickering on the wall, the sound of a bird or a siren. Nonthinking is accompanied by intensified awareness.

This unfettered, unstoppable mind is what informs all of our activity. It is not confined to the sitting position; we have to try to get up without leaving this awareness. So, when we finish our practice, we stretch gently and with slow, mindful movements we get up. We try not to lose awareness of our breath or the relationship between our head and shoulders. We stand up and, with our feet reaching into the ground like a tree's roots, we take our place. We straighten our posture. On the out-breath we take a half step forward. Each successive out-breath is accompanied by a half step forward. We slow down our walking and our habitual movements and bring awareness to the process. We don't try to be this or that, or walk like this or that; we simply follow the formula and observe closely.

From here we can move into our daily life. The breath and the posture give us touchstones to return to basic sanity, clarity, and spacious mind. Once this becomes familiar it feels like returning home or finding a refuge. It is best to cultivate this practice with regularity and discipline. One way is to sandwich the day with meditation, morning and evening.

DEDICATE YOUR MERIT

To fully realize the View, we dedicate the merit of our actions. This is an idea taken from Buddhism.

If we have designed a garden from the point of view of helping all beings who enter and enjoy it, if we have taken into account the needs of the client and of the land and have designed a place of peace and repose, this is a big deal. We have done something worth doing, both in the practical sense and in the spiritual realm. The same is true if we have worked to implement design principles and vision into our daily lives and relationships.

But accomplishing something worthwhile, while it may make us happy, should also help others. The simple fact of creating a garden that respects the environment it sits in and suits the needs of its users will please our clients and all those who use the garden. But the merit of doing this should not simply redound to our own egos or reputations as garden designers; it should be used to renew our efforts to do more deeds like this in the world. It should spur our desire to create spaces that delight and serve those who enter them. So we dedicate the merit we've accumulated to those ends.

Dedication of merit need not be some huge ceremony or outward display. Instead, we simply offer the benefit we've created for the enhancement of the lives of all beings. It helps to have some sort of formula for this, and each designer has her own words or gestures that will signify dedication for them. Personally, I use a traditional verse:

By this merit, may all obtain omniscience.
May it defeat the enemy, wrongdoing.
From the stormy waves of birth, old age, sickness, and death,
May we free all beings.

This dedication frees us from egotistical contamination of our work. Thus, we reaffirm our altruistic motivation and remain humble.

THE PROCESS

Poem 2

Sitting in the darkness
Nothing more to gain
Nothing more to lose
Sometimes laughing
Sometimes crying
Sometimes nothing at all—
Listening.

—Martin Mosko

Once the concept of the garden is clearly understood and the View established, we can begin to focus on the elements of our design. First, we clearly define our design goals—what we want the garden to accomplish. It may be that we want to make sick people feel better or that we want to improve the city dweller's access to nature. There are always practical considerations to be addressed, like drainage and exposure. And there are the needs and desires of the client to take into account, including how they want the garden to feel and how they plan to make use of it. But if these are the only things we consider, the garden will be nothing more than a decoration of the space. We want the garden to be a place pregnant with potential for realization. This section explores the aspects of design that can make this possible.

EXAMINE THE ENVIRONMENT
WITHOUT PROJECTIONS

Once we understand our design goals and have calmed our mind with meditation, we next turn outward, to listen to the land and to ourselves. It's important to recognize that our projections distort our perceptions and our pictures of reality, so we open ourselves to fresh observation when we begin this stage of design.

If you are observing carefully and with an open mind, you can assess your environment without prejudice or judgment. If we want to change our lives or environment, we start with understanding their current condition. If we're going to improve our business operations, for example, we first develop a clear idea of what works and what doesn't. If we want to improve our lives, we do the same.

In the garden, we begin with the land. The garden is not designed in the abstract. It is spirit manifesting on earth in a specific location at a specific time. We need to fully understand the terrain: its contours, texture, and inhabitants. There are two aspects to this: getting to know the site physically and energetically, and doing research about its conditions. Generally speaking, the more time we spend on the site, the better. A colleague of mine measures the site by hand and always makes his own topographic map. This requires a careful understanding of the site's boundaries, relationships, and nuances. We can understand these elements intellectually from a topographical survey, but we need to know the site on a cellular level.

As with any kind of design, we begin with careful, unbiased research. The more we know about the existing conditions the better.

It is important that we understand as much as we can about the background of the environment. What is the history of the climate in the vicinity of the garden? What is it predicted to become? How cold can it get? And how hot? How much rainfall and/or snow is there per year? How much can come in a single storm event? What is the average wind speed, and what are the historical extremes? What are the direction and intensity of the wind as indicated by the trees? What is the ecology of the site? How does it relate to its environment? Is it part of a mountain lion's territory? Are there precious, perhaps endangered, plants on site? What are the drainage patterns? Are there animal tracks? What are the opportunities inherent in the site and what are the challenges?

We should understand not only the site, but also its surroundings and how the two relate. Is the site surrounded by a wall and entered through a gate or is the boundary a hedge? Are there intrusive views, sounds, or odors? Are there opportunities for borrowed scenery like a mountain, a tree, a breeze? Where does the sun rise at the winter solstice and where at the summer solstice? Where are the shadows from neighboring structures or trees in the existing site?

I once designed a courtyard garden for people who had hired a famous Italian architect to design their home. I'm not sure how familiar he was with the site, but the resulting building opened the central courtyard to a howling wind that screamed down a nearby canyon and swept through the area intended for a garden. We had to design a garden, but we also had to design a clear glass wall that was installed at one corner where the wind blasted through. Only after we dealt with the wind issue could the garden building continue. This is the cost of ignoring the landscape surrounding the garden. We always consider how the landscape and the garden will affect each other.

Once we know all that we can and have internalized the qualities of the site, we turn our attention to its hidden dimensions. We dig test holes throughout the site to see what the soil is like. We then need to take soil samples wherever we find variation and have them analyzed. We ought to know the acidity and alkalinity of the soil, its mineral and microbial content, whether or not it is expansive, and how easily water and air will pass through it. We also examine the water source and know its quality.

After we have thoroughly explored the physical characteristics of the site, we examine the energetic structure of the land. During the workshops we teach, we ask participants to find the primary, secondary, and tertiary "power spots" on the site. In almost all cases there is agreement on what and where these are. These spots are where we might locate a pavilion, a bench, a center of focus, a rock arrangement, a waterfall, a pond, and the like. They are the places we either want to look at or look from. The survey cannot give us this information. Only by intimately knowing the site do we sense where these strategic locations are.

I want to emphasize the importance of knowing the land, looking with clarity and attention at what is there, looking with unfiltered seeing. Know the land like you know your body. Understand its physiology, its psychology, and its spirit. This takes time. Don't compromise on this part of the process. Do all the research thoroughly. It will prove indispensable as we move into the design process.

Often it is easier to do this when we work as a team. The homeowner may have useful observations to share with us about what happens when there is heavy rain or snow, how the birds feed in the trees, or how far the shadow of the house falls in different seasons. An experienced engineer may have valuable input about the state of a wall, and an arborist may be able to contribute information about the health of the major trees on site. Even with an open mind, we cannot always see everything by ourselves.

This is true in every aspect of our lives. Business consultants make a living by being a trained set of new eyes on a situation, and they can often spot the root of problems that those immersed in the day-to-day operations don't have the perspective to see. We rely on mentors and teachers in our work and hobbies, we use athletic trainers when we are learning a new sport or trying to get back into shape. These are all examples of how an outside observer can help us put our lives in order.

This is also why we can learn from our spiritual teachers. As many texts or books as we read, as much meditation as we might do, and as sincere as our practice might be, we can still meet obstacles and difficulties that occur because we can't see ourselves or our situations clearly. In certain Buddhist traditions, the teacher is called a "spiritual friend," someone who has your best interests at heart and who can see your life from a different angle. A caring and observant teacher can be beneficial as we try to assess our lives as they are.

———

CONSIDER YOUR CONSTRAINTS
AND LEARN TO CREATE WITHIN THEM

In any undertaking, there are constraints. The garden designer, like the poet or the musician, chooses a form and is creative within it. The painter chooses the size of the canvas, the accountant operates within generally accepted principles, the businessperson accepts limits on capital or bank restrictions on activities. It is simply working with reality to recognize the limits that will be placed on our work and learning to operate within them.

There are always going to be constraints on the garden designer, and these give shape to the initial design. The first of these might be access to the site. This is important because it will influence what kind and weight of materials we can use. Large boulders don't go through narrow gates, for example. Restricted access limits possible alternatives to design and influences the planning of the construction. If the site can only be accessed from one location, the garden will have to be started from the point most distant from that access and built toward the access point. On one project, we had to build from the two ends toward the middle, then back our way out. This was especially challenging because we built a river running the length of the garden.

Materials are another constraint. What plants are available? There may be a wide variety of plants that will grow in the soil and the climate, but it may not be practical to obtain them. In addition to the practical concerns, there may be ethical questions, for instance, about planting an invasive species. Plants native to one area may be inappropriate somewhere else. This is particularly true in the dry American southwest, where there is a growing effort to replace lawns with xeric plants, which use much less water.

The question is the same for using other materials like metals, boulders, paving stones, concrete, and so on. A garden is built with what is available. For example, it may not be practical to add large boulders to a design if there is no quarry nearby.

Other constraints are skilled labor and machinery. This can be overcome if the budget allows. Skilled craftsmen travel, and machinery and operators do as well. I once did a job near a Marine training base, and all the available landscape laborers were former Marines. They had no idea what I was creating, but they had the right equipment and, most importantly, they had the right attitude. I've been in other situations where we had the right boulders but not the equipment to move them or set them.

Budget is always a constraint. I've never had a project that didn't have a budget, and even when the budget was large, it was never unlimited. My approach has often been to create a design that suits the land and the owner's vision and comes at least close to the budget they have in mind. If the vision and the direction are quite clear, then it's possible to review the design when the costs have been determined and figure out what can be cut without damaging the overall integrity of the design.

Laws, covenants, and customs are important constraints. We can't build an eight-foot wall if the town covenants only allow six-foot walls. We may not be allowed to obstruct a neighboring view. There may be limitations on the water we can use. There can be restrictions on how structures are built, what they are made of, and what color they can be. There may be requirements to plant a certain number of trees and a restricted list of allowable plants. There may also be drainage limitations; for example, perhaps no water can be allowed to drain off of the site or it must drain in a specific direction.

Also, there are social, cultural, and historical constraints. The garden may be in a historical district, which can severely limit what can and cannot be done. If you are working in a maritime zone or a watershed district, you will have to research what is or isn't allowed. Some imagery or metaphors may be obscure or offensive to some people. Different ethnicities and age groups use garden space differently. This is not an explicit constraint, but requires sensitivity.

There may be time constraints. The project may have to follow a certain time line and the design decisions made to accord with this. Since design is a process, it is important to allow time for not only the design work itself but presentations and iterations. Everything depends on proper scheduling. The downside is that since everything is in a state of change, the unpredictable is about the only thing that's predictable. The schedule has to be constantly modified and reevaluated. Everyone should be aware of changes as they happen.

We might wish the budget or space were bigger or that more time had been allocated for the project, but good design is about working within constraints. Constraints are not bad things; they are part of the very nature of the art, and all constraints can be opportunities.

––––––

ORGANIZE YOUR MATERIALS IN COHERENT PATTERNS

As we learn about the garden site, we are considering how we will put the elements into some kind of order and where they will go in relationship with one another and with the land. Because each element has its own energy and meaning, each has to be incorporated into the design in a coherent way.

The garden is an overlay of many complex systems (environmental, ecological, biological, chemical, metaphorical, energetic) and complex formal relationships (proportional, rhythmical, numerical, spatial). We can use this complexity to create and sustain multiple layers of beauty and meaning. However, it is easy to overload the design and turn everything into a blur.

When designing, we should strip away everything that is not necessary, reducing the design to the greatest degree of simplicity without compromising its inherent integrity. Even the simplest design will have more going on than we are able to follow.

In the garden we are encouraged to slow down and take time with our perceptions and our awareness. We don't want to feel any competition for our attention. We want each vignette to be simple and unified and to quiet the mind.

Simplicity allows the viewer to exercise imagination. When we see a three-stone arrangement, for example, it will evoke different things for different people, but each will bring his own experience and perspective to the view. As designers, this is exactly what we hope to accomplish: to draw the viewer into a relationship with the materials and to discover their sense of the sacred.

The garden wants to share itself. Without overwhelming or demanding too much attention, it should allow relaxation and space for insight and realization. Simplicity draws our attention to details and allows us to appreciate subtlety. Quiet gives us encouragement to find our own rhythm.

———

CONNECT HEAVEN, EARTH, AND MAN

The volume of the garden contains what is beneath us and above us, and what is in between. In a building this would be the floor, the ceiling, and the walls. The floor is the basis, where our feet rest. It is the foundation, the place from which all scale and proportion begin. The limit of the vertical axis is the ceiling, the overhead element. Together with the wall element, which connects floor to ceiling, it defines volume and mass. This floor/wall/ceiling categorization is often used in both architecture and landscape architecture, and it can be studied in any textbook.

Contemplative design adds a profundity to this structure. We call this relationship among the physical elements the coming together of Heaven, Earth, and Man. This is what makes the difference in contemplative design, or for that matter contemplative life: observing the profound within the mundane and giving voice to it in our work.

Most of us have a feeling of the divine coming from the above. Primitive man saw that there was an order to the movement of planets and constellations and from that order decided that the sky was a space inhabited by gods. Even now, many offer incense or burn fires to give the deities a route down via the smoke to our earthly presence. So for the garden designer, this overhead element is the Heaven element. It is the divine presence we seek to marry with the Earth.

Heaven, in this understanding of physical relationships, is what is overhead: the sky, the tree, the trellis, the roof. The overhead controls sunlight. A grove of palm trees gives a filtered light, protecting us from the tropical sun and at the same time revealing a balance of light and dark on the ground. The same may apply to a trellis, which filters light, or a full roof, which completely blocks all light. All of these—the tree, the trellis, and the roof—give us a feeling of protection and safety. If what is overhead is out of balance, with too much Heaven element, we might feel that the environment is dark and oppressive. This is not always a bad thing. We might want to create that feeling to lead to a vast, open, dreamlike vista. The oppressiveness of the dark passageway accentuates the expansive feeling of the open, light-filled garden view.

The ground plane is the Earth element. Our entire world is part of this matrix. Earth is the hardscape, the flower beds and ground covers, ponds and fire pits. It is the floor of garden structures, the base of sculptures, the steps, and the pathways. Earth is the foundation from which everything arises.

In designing with the Earth element, we have to be sure that it does not overwhelm the other elements. Once we visited a landscape architecture school and were invited to review some of the students' final projects. One young man showed us his design for an elaborate private backyard garden, complete with a pool, fire pit, and extensive stroll gardens with pathways meandering through them. He was stymied because with all of these features, he still felt the garden was somehow incomplete. He had no Heaven element to balance the Earth element. There was nothing overhead at all: no trees, no arbor, no sheltering overhang from the house. I suggested he reconsider his design in that light.

Joining Heaven and Earth is Man. It might be a shrub, a boulder, a mound, a bench, or a gate. We call it the Man element because the human scale defines the proportionate relationships of this trait. When designing a garden, it is particularly important to understand where our eye level is in relation to the garden elements. This is the basis for understanding vertical proportions. Is the shrub eight feet high, three feet above eye level? Is it three feet high, two feet below eye level? Proportion is considered relative to eye level, and scale has to do with how far each element is from the viewer. An eight-foot stone that is two feet from the viewer is quite a different experience of scale than a stone that is eight feet high and twenty feet from the viewer.

The Man element has mass and manages the view. It might frame a view between two shrubs, obscure a view, or reveal a view with a hole or a window. It can create mystery. Passing through a hedgerow on both sides with the end hidden by another shrub, we have no idea what will be revealed at the end of the passage.

The relationship among Heaven, Earth, and Man is fundamental in contemplative design. It can be applied to rock setting, plant design, and many relationships in the garden space. Each element has to be present in order for the garden to feel complete and balanced.

ACHIEVE A NATURAL SENSE OF FLOW

Another important consideration when arranging the elements is flow. When we look at a garden, our eyes should move smoothly in a manner choreographed by the designer through the use of visual elements. Likewise, walking through the garden should be an organic and comfortable experience. We might call this the music of the garden, or how the parts sing together as a whole to create an impression that is intentional and coherent.

A proper sense of flow is part of every kind of design, whether it be for a garden or a retail store or a highway system. Paying attention to this experience of flow, visual or kinesthetic, improves every type of design.

The garden designer works with structure and shapes, colors, directions, patterns, and rhythm to create flow. The flow contains both movement and stillness, and each is included in the design.

Shape

The shape of each element can stop the eye, startle us into stillness, or allow us to move smoothly onto the next element. For example, a large triangle (a rock or a shrub in the shape of a triangle) will often bring us up short. It is an unexpected natural shape that will make us pause either visually or physically. It is a static kind of element that will interrupt flow. This can be an excellent design tool when we want to arrest the attention of the garden visitor.

The size and shape of various elements, like plants or rocks, can fit together to form a small picture or vignette, or they can work against each other and feel strange and out of place. If a giant boulder towers over surrounding ground-cover plants, it will draw the eye to a full stop. Again, this is beneficial when the designer wants to call attention to a significant feature, such as a sculpture, or wants to mark a particular point in the garden, like an entryway. This may work against us if the idea is to enjoy a continuing journey toward a destination, such as a beach, a view, or a patio.

Color

Color is another part of flow. In one garden I created, there were five individual spaces built around single colors. Each space had a different feel and emotional quality. We don't usually have the luxury of this amount of space, but it's important that we understand how each color works in order to evoke certain responses.

Color is an integral part of form, not separate from it or added to it. Color and form both have resonance in our emotional and archetypal memories. Rocks have color. Pathways have color. Dark shades of umber and gray are a perfect background for the exhibitionist peony. Color evokes memory: Maybe our mother favored a specific color, or we remember the color of the walls in our childhood bedroom. When we see that color in a flower, the flower brings back the memory of our mother, or of our youth, along with the emotions involved. These associations are an important part of creating a connection between garden and viewer.

The meaning of colors goes beyond an individual's personal response. The five basic colors have archetypal homes in the emotional configuration of consciousness:

- Yellow or gold signifies fruition and ripening. It is the color of autumn. Its energy is exuberant, expansive, and rich.
- Blue is the color of the sky and the sky reflected in water. It signifies wisdom, precision, clear vision. Its energy is like that of a diamond.
- Red is the color of primal energy. The red rose means romance. The energy of red is magnetizing. It is the color of fire, and the color of heat.
- Green is the color of activity, with energy like the wind. It is the color of summer, the green grasses and meadows, the forest in its fullness, the business of life generated by the warmth of sunshine.
- White is the color of clarity and purity. It is emblematic of emptiness, the absence of all color, and it expresses all-pervading space.

A thorough investigation of the colors and energies of the Buddha families can be found in Irini Rockwell's book *The Five Wisdom Energies*.

We can use the tools of color and shape to create pattern and rhythm in the flow of the garden.

Pattern

Recurring patterns can evoke feelings that help to express the poetry of the garden. For example, a highly structured French garden or an English "knot" garden will be static. These gardens are often designed to be viewed rather than walked through, and give a sense of order. They are built around a central axis that defines a symmetrical pattern with each half a mirror of the other.

Asymmetry, a characteristic of Japanese gardens, has its own effect. The idealized mandala may have an exact geometry, but when it manifests on earth it departs from the grid, the axis, and the stasis. It is an open system that allows for growth and change as well as individual interpretation and private realization. It is more poetry than geometry. Evoking this rich and sensually compelling kind of space may mean using shapes that are not quite round, not quite square, not quite straight.

We create patterns with rocks, plants, pathways, and so on. Plant patterns are generated by their color, texture, size, form, behavior, species, and ecological similarities. Stones can have patterns based on their geology, size, texture, color, and form. So when we think about creating a mandala of interrelated patterns, we first need to decide what elements we want to use in the organization.

A motif is a repetitive use of pattern. There are formal motifs and irregular motifs. Some formal motifs are radial, linear array, triangular, or circular array, or an array based on any mathematical progression, such as the Fibonacci series, the golden mean, unfolding random sequences, and so on. Irregular motifs are recurring patterns that vary in size and proportion and appear in the garden in a seemingly random way.

Rhythm

The garden designer works with patterns, or the repetition of discrete elements, to create rhythm. Regular rhythms are easily absorbed and can be reassuring to the viewer. Broken or off-beat rhythms can be compelling, drawing upon our curiosity and challenging our capacity to find order. Rhythm is an ordering of parts mathematically. Just as there might be four beats in a measure of music, likewise there can be four plants in a sequence, and the sequence can be repeated regularly, or not. Just as in music, rhythm in the garden can be used to create emphasis. If in a measure of music a certain beat is accented, it sets a pace for the song. This can be done just as easily with garden elements. If a rhythm is created with yellow plants, for example, the flow can have accents defined by size or mass or volume. This adds lyricism to the design.

Rhythm is also the movement between like elements. The mind seeks sensory patterns and sorts them with rhythm. This is particularly noticeable when the rhythm is regular. There are three different kinds of rhythm: visual, auditory, and kinesthetic. Each of these is important to garden design.

One example of visual rhythm is a repeated use of a globe-shaped shrub in the garden, which causes our eye to move from one shrub to the other (though not usually in a straight line). If we are looking at the garden from a viewing platform, our eye might travel from the globe shrub on our left up to the one on a mound just to the right and then to another maybe on a lower mound farther to the right and then perhaps to the one in the foreground. This eye movement is a visual rhythm.

Visual rhythm is also a factor as we move along a path. If we see these globe spruces as we proceed along a path, each time one appears it will relate as a pattern to the ones that have gone before and the time in which they make their appearances will be experienced as a rhythm.

Auditory rhythm is usually created with water sounds. We might hear the babbling of a creek as we are walking along a path and then lose its sound as we proceed, only to pick it up again as we turn a corner. We might also hear the sound our feet make as they move along a path, giving us a measure of the rhythm of our walking. Adding steppers or obstacles in the path can syncopate this rhythm.

Kinesthetic rhythm is the felt experience of the garden in our bodies. The experience of a particular walking surface, if repeated systematically, creates a kinesthetic rhythm. Repetition of cool and moist areas or hot and dry environments offers a kinesthetic rhythm. The textures of plants as they are repeated through the garden give a sensibility that can be felt.

———

ARRANGE MATERIALS TO HEIGHTEN AWARENESS

Normally our minds are full of clutter and noise—I have to do this or that or I have to be here or there—and we walk around in a cocoon, unaware of our own separation from reality. This condition of a noisy and cluttered mind is the opposite of heightened awareness.

Every environment either fosters this distraction or serves to reduce it. Wherever we spend our time—whether in our office, our kitchen, or our car—everything around us affects our emotional responses and the degree of our awareness. We have a friend whose computer is programmed to chime every twenty minutes to bring him back to the present moment and break up patterns of physical stillness and mental wandering. When the chime sounds, our friend stands, stretches, breathes deeply, and finds himself refreshed and present once more.

The garden designer uses the materials of the garden to help us slow down and return to our center, allowing the mind to settle, like the mud that settles out of water once the agitation has stopped. The more that the garden forces us to slow down, take our time, and enjoy the journey through it, the greater the opportunity for the mind to clear and to surrender to something larger than its busy chatter. There are a number of means to do this, but all of them rely on heightening our sensual experiences and awareness; they are outlined below.

Boundaries and Thresholds

One of the first considerations of the design is its boundary, which is the limit of what we will define as the garden and the canvas for the design. The boundary should be more than simply the edge of the garden, the line where it peters out. The more definition and clarity we can give to the boundary, the greater the sense of an enclosed world. The boundary becomes the skin of the garden, encompassing and enhancing its energy system. A walled garden can turn a desert into an oasis and a chaotic city into a sanctuary.

Boundaries do not have to be walls or solid fences, though of course they may be. They can be a screen of trees, a berm, a knee-high picket fence, a hedge, or a trellised vine. Anything that helps to define the space will make it feel more enclosed and protected. When we feel safe and contained, we can relax, we can completely exhale.

The threshold, the moment of entering the boundary of the garden, is also important. Coming in through a garden gate or an arbor immediately establishes a feeling of going from one place to another and allows us to drop the baggage we carried with us on the way into the garden.

Since water, of all the natural elements, most closely resembles the nature of mind, bridges have a special meaning. They represent passing from one place to another, one state of mind to another, perhaps from a condition of distraction to one of alertness. In bridge design we consider a number of factors. Does it activate the imagination so that it does far more than get us from here to there? Does it transport us from one state of being to another? Is it a symbol of transformation?

We design bridges more for the imagination than for their functionality. Just think of Monet's garden at Giverny—what would it be without the bridge? Some bridges are not meant to be traversed by foot, only by the mind connecting here and there.

Conceal and Reveal

Conceal and reveal is a means of constantly creating heightened awareness as we journey through the garden. The contemplative designer imagines a path and the experience of moving along it. With every few steps, something we've just seen is concealed and some new picture, smell, or sound is revealed. When the rhythms of constantly changing beauty are carefully composed, our journey on the garden path brings us into the present moment. As long as the views are compelling, we can't ignore the fleeting and precious experience they offer, and we are drawn away from our problems, our worries, and our mental conspiracies into the delight of the moment.

There are many methods that allow us to conceal the old and reveal the new. Height is one way. Anything higher than an average eye level of five feet will conceal what is beyond. So we could add a large shrub, a small tree, a landform, a rock arrangement, or some combination of these to separate different views from one another. Movement is another way to do this. We can twist the path around these objects so that the journey continually presents us with something new to see. Some larger gardens are divided into "rooms" by hedges, trees, or other forms, with each room having its own features, color palette, and seating. In designing a stroll garden it is best to use this technique liberally. Every few steps can reveal a new, magnetizing vista.

Steppers/Stairs

Another means of heightening awareness is by slowing people down as they move through the garden. We can do this by requiring their careful attention as they move along the paths of the garden. I often use stone steppers with gaps between them; people automatically try to step only on the stones and not in the gaps. The more visually interesting you can make these, the more that you can engage the walker. The Japanese are masters of this, using varied types of stone, gravel, wood rounds, and other tricks to keep us focused on the moment of walking.

Stairs also slow people down. Though public spaces require ramps as alternate paths, in most settings irregular stairs will force people to slow down, to pay attention as they climb. If the stairway turns, or if the top view is obscured either by the grade or by plants, the stairway draws people upward to see what might be at the top.

In a garden I visited in Japan, the pathway led through a shady wood, with very little view beyond the surrounding trees. The stairs near the end of the path led upward and turned, so you had no idea what was ahead. At the topmost riser, there appeared a broad vista across a large pond, sun-filled and bright after the darker wood. The surprise was breathtaking and certainly pulled you into the present moment (as well as rewarding you for climbing all those stairs).

Contrast and Chiaroscuro

Finally, contrast is another way to heighten awareness in the garden. We classify phenomena by contrast. We know black because of white, long because of short, near because of far, pain because of pleasure, life because of death. Definitions are strongest and clearest when the contrast is most extreme. The designer uses contrast to influence how we perceive. This is done in two ways: through color and through light.

When selecting color, we think in terms of contrast. If we have high contrast, we increase our perception of the separateness of things; if we have low contrast, we tone down the visual differences between all things. If the color value of the flowers is the same as that of the leaves, then the color of the flowers no longer jumps out at you and asks to be noticed. If we want a yellow flower to be noticed, we create a high contrast by surrounding it with red flowers or white ones. If we want to experience yellowness without particular distinction, we create a low contrast by making a field of yellow flowers.

Chiaroscuro is the application of contrast between light and shade. Here we are referring to light and the degree of luminosity. When considering light, it is as though we need to discount the effects of saturation and vibrancy. When we do, we are left with the contrast of light and dark. When that contrast is extreme, objects have clear distinction; when the contrast is slight, objects blend together. This is easily understood by looking at a black-and-white photograph. The movement of the eye and what it notices is largely a result of the contrast between black and white and the hundreds of shades of gray in between. Chiaroscuro can be applied with any color, but it is most effective when the color is restrained and limited. If we add color, the chiaroscuro is still there, but not nearly as prominently. Italian gardens, which make extensive use of chiaroscuro, usually employ a limited color palette. Japanese gardens are similar in this respect.

The relationship between light and dark is also how we perceive volume, which in turn is how we see distance and space. Think of a light shining on a sphere: If the light is directly in front of the sphere, it will look like a circle. If the light source moves, the shadows cast by the sphere will make it clear that it is a three-dimensional object. As we change the background of the object from light to dark, we get more contrast and therefore more prominence. Contrast is critical to creating emphasis and also critical to avoid when we don't want emphasis.

Chiaroscuro, which changes minute by minute in the garden when the illumination is the sun, contributes to our sense of the garden as ephemeral, momentary, and passing. Even large boulders will be affected by this continual change in light, and the designer can use this to change the mood or feeling throughout the day.

ENGAGE THE IMAGINATION OF THE VIEWER

As we design a garden, we are trying to create a space that engages the minds and hearts of those who enter it, to give them freedom from their mental chatter and openness to things greater than the small self. The designer can use analogies and metaphors in order to accomplish this.

The human mind is constantly searching for meaningful patterns. This is a survival mechanism; it helps us see the skin of the tiger against the dappled light coming through the trees or the edges of a pathway that someone has created to lead us to safety. As designers, we can appeal to that instinctive mind by creating arrangements of materials that suggest meaning to those who see them.

For example, when I design in the garden, I like to use patterns that metaphorically shape an animal or a king and his court. Even if people can't see what I see in the arrangement, they will sense the pattern and imbue it with their own meaning. These metaphors help us to relate to the environment of the garden, and generate a sense of connection to it.

While building a garden in South Carolina, I was unable to be there for setting the stones. I explained to the contractor that he should organize the stones I had selected according to some meaningful metaphor, like a mother and her children, a swarm of bees, a school of fish, or whatever made sense to him in a profound way. He pondered this for a bit and then said, "I've got it. I'll make a male alligator chasing a female alligator." I told him that would be perfect. When we experience the garden, we probably don't see the "alligators," but we sense an order. It might not be a mathematical order, but it somehow makes sense to us.

The garden is an interconnected system. If we remove a rock, it changes the feeling of the rock arrangement as well as the plants that surround it or the water that flows around it. The better integrated the materials of the garden, the clearer these relationships are.

By analogy, this allows viewers the opportunity to more fully understand the interconnections in their own lives. For instance, the effects of anger, pride, greed, and jealousy shape our lives and since, like the garden, everything is interconnected, the ramifications go far beyond what we can see or know.

Although each element of the garden is connected to all the others, each is an individual. That rock we are removing exists in relation to the other rocks, plants, and water, but it also exists as an important element itself. If the designer has chosen the material well, we can appreciate the rock's unique qualities and its appearance as an interesting element on its own. The viewer who can appreciate this can see that she, too, exists as an individual, with an important role as herself in her family and society.

The power of the metaphors and symbols used in garden design come in large part from their ability to stir the imagination and memories of those who experience them. Even widely understood representations will not necessarily spark the same associations with all people. Every visitor brings to the garden her own cultural and emotional history and will see things in her own way. Far from being a drawback, the opportunity to elicit a different meaning from everyone who experiences a garden is a powerful aspect of building one. There are always layers of meaning, both obvious and unseen, in any design. For example, a pond to me represents Buddha nature, our basic clear and luminous mind that is neither created nor destroyed. For another designer, perhaps the pond is the re-creation of the water next to which he had an epiphany some years ago. This layers the design with direct experience.

The garden is a physical space, with boundaries around the elements that comprise it. But it is equally an emotional and imaginative space that we fill in with our associations to the elements used and the particular ways in which they're arranged. So if you create a three-stone arrangement that you mean to represent Heaven, Earth, and Man, others will connect with that arrangement, but it can mean something different to them. Perhaps they will see the Christian trinity or a family of father, mother, and child. In some sense, the meaning of the arrangement is more powerful the more abstract it is because it allows for individual interpretation. Each of these interpretations is as powerful and meaningful as all the others.

USE VISUALIZATION AS THE STRUCTURE OF CONTEMPLATIVE DESIGN

With an understanding of our design goals, the land, and the possibilities inherent in the elements that make up the land, we can begin visualizing the garden we want to create. Visualization is a technique that brings meditation together with the information we gather in our research of the land and the client or our own needs. It's an important part of the garden design process and a very useful tool to employ in other aspects of our lives.

Let's begin with how to use the technique in garden design. Once we have fully absorbed our knowledge of the land, that information enters the field of our consciousness, and an alchemical process takes place. What was substantial and material is now purely a thought form, a memory, an imagining. When we see that the external world is as imaginary as the mentally visualized world, we free our creative minds to mix what is with what might be, joining Heaven and Earth, mind and matter, spirit and substance.

Before trying to visualize an entire garden design, we might begin with something simple like visualizing an orange or an apple in the space in front of us. Place the actual fruit in front of you close to eye level and look at it with an unwavering gaze. After a while, close your eyes and see if you can see the fruit in your mind's eye. Open your eyes and notice what your imagined image was missing. Did you visualize the shadows, the color gradients, and textures? Close your eyes and bring up the image again.

It may help you to picture the fruit on an imagined x, y, z grid with the center at the very bottom of the orange. Projecting axes onto the object of visualization gives us a means of examining relative sizes and proportions of objects, and it gives us a way to explore the distances between multiple objects and their effect from the viewer's vantage point.

Another technique I find helpful is to make a drawing of the object of contemplation. Look with unwavering gaze at the object, then close your eyes and visualize the object. Open your eyes and without looking at the object, draw it. Reexamine the object and compare it to your drawing. Perhaps use the axes to see this in greater detail. Close your eyes again and reimagine the object. Open your eyes and redraw it. This time try to project your mental image onto the page and see it first, then trace it. I find that this helps me to see the object in my mind's eye with greater and greater clarity.

If you can't see the object clearly as a whole, focus on a small part of it. Look at its relation to the table or floor. See its textures, the movement of light across its surface, the way it responds to gravity. Sometimes by starting with a fragment, we stabilize our seeing and can then gradually add to it until the whole fruit is in our projected view.

I find that visualization can be easier if visualizing a sacred image, such as a painting of the Buddha, or an object that has emotional content, like a picture of my children. Instead of visualizing this object on the x, y, z axes and carefully observing the way light reveals form, we might focus on the feeling of being in the presence of this object. For me, this is very useful. The picture evolves from the stabilized feeling of the space. Of course, not everyone projects in the same way.

If we practice looking closely at things, we'll begin to understand the nature of visual perception. We'll notice how we tend to label what we see and then fail to see the thing itself at all. We say, "Oh, that's an orange," and once it has a name we lose our perceptual connection with it. So we try to see the object of contemplation before it has a name. To do this we might have to work through habitual mental patterns that stand between our seeing, the object, and true perception.

This is a very important practice for contemplative design. It is also an extremely important practice for cultivating true perception. The truth is, we rarely see our world as it is. We overlay our so-called reality with our story line, our version of what is and how things are. The Buddha says that all human suffering comes from not seeing things as they are. Until we correct this we cannot embrace true seeing, and without true perception, there cannot be a true view or connection with the way in which things actually exist.

Once you have some practice with visualizing simple things, you can move to visualizing the garden design. First, sit in a quiet place and calm your mind. Then, maintaining correct posture and a relaxed mind, visualize the garden site as it is. Remove from the visualization all unnecessary elements (e.g., most of the plant material, rocks, even the current topography), retaining only those which you have compelling reasons to keep, such as an old tree, a sacred grove, the drainage, or anything the client specifically wants to retain in the design. (Remember that any plant material you keep will limit what you can do with the grade around it.) In your mind, you can move around and through the visualization. We stabilize the visualization in this condition. Once you have this base, you can add more detail, like the sun, its shadow, its warmth, the direction of the light, and whatever details add to experiencing the space.

Next, visualize something sacred to you in this space. I visualize Buddha, the form of wakefulness and compassion, and I ask this visualization to show how it wants to manifest in the garden space. We are asking Buddha or the spirit of the land or the divine (whatever means the most to you) to manifest as mountains, valleys, and groves of trees, waterfalls, rivers, ponds, and flowers.

Overlay this sense of the sacred onto the land and begin to visualize the garden design in the space. Sometimes the whole garden appears at once, in complete detail. At this time a name for the garden often appears. Other times it emerges slowly like a morning mist clearing from a valley. I explore the visualized garden space and begin to see where the pathways are and where they go and how the boulders are arranged. Continue to fill in the visualization. The water is next. It is thoroughly interconnected with the rockwork. Then visualize the plants and see how they might relate to the land, the rock, and the water.

Another approach to visualization is to let the imagination walk through the garden. Imagine the entrance, the opening to an intimate and sacred world. What does it look like? How does it feel to pass through the gate or the threshold? What sense of mystery is awakened? What adventures and explorations await us? What discoveries?

Then imagine the location of the power spots and see yourself walking along a pathway from the entrance to one of these. What is on your left? What is on your right? Do you see the destination? If it is hidden, what conceals it and how? Is it sunny or shaded? Try to feel yourself in the space as you move very slowly through it.

Whatever techniques help you to create the vision of the garden, do not rush through them. Allow the vision to emerge. I've sat with the base image for long, long hours with nothing appearing in my mind's eye. I wait and wait and wait, always keeping the image stabilized. Eventually, the garden appears.

Once we can stabilize a vision of the garden, we notice that our mental picture occurs in a specific light and time of day. This is either the time when we visited and studied the land or perhaps the time when we took our set of "before" photos. Since our garden lives through all the seasons, we manipulate the visualization. In your mind's eye, advance the vision of the garden in time, throughout the year, throughout the seasons, to be sure that what you have in mind will work during all of those periods.

This process takes time and patience, but for the designer seeking to join Heaven and Earth, it is a necessary, fundamental skill. It is the doorway to a memory bank far beyond our personal experience.

The visualization technique can be applied to any of your goals. Once you know what you are aiming for in your life, you can visualize yourself achieving those goals. This will produce both a positive frame of mind (which allows us to be more spontaneous and clear) and an encouraging support when we tire. Visualization gives us a taste of success as we make changes to ourselves along the way. For example, if you want to be more generous, visualize clearly how that would feel in your body, what the external environment would be that would promote that feeling, and how your emotions would respond if you felt that you'd been able to perform a generous act. If you can keep this clear vision in mind, you can have something to remind you how to act and react in various situations that will result in a greater degree of generosity.

Another use of visualization is to imagine various outcomes of a difficult situation you're facing. If you can visualize a positive result, it may assist you in figuring out what steps you'll have to take in order to achieve it. Are you going to confront a coworker about some issue between you? Visualize the outcome you want—better communication, more cooperation, less harassment—and examine that visualization. It will give you clues on how to manage the discussion more fruitfully and to see the conflict from the other side.

We can use visualization to understand our futures as well. Suppose you are in a job that's not making you happy. Use your best sense of where you are now—how you spend your time, what people are around you, what you like and don't like about the job. Then visualize where you'll be in five years, and what you'll be doing. What will the rhythm of your day be like, and who are the people you'll be working with? Will you have a greater degree of satisfaction or less? If you project what that future holds, you can better understand what, if any, changes you should make in the present in order to improve that visualization.

The gardener also uses this kind of projected visualization. In order to trim the trees or cultivate the flower beds or keep up the path, we start by visualizing what the tree would ideally look like in a few years. What plants would take over the space if they are left untended? Where should the paths be mended, or shrubs cut back, to keep them clear?

EVALUATE THE DESIGN AND ADAPT IT TO THE VISION

Once the vision of the design manifests as a working document, everyone can see it, examine it, imagine it, and evaluate it. The View is the common language of evaluation. It gives us the way to talk about the merit of the contemplative garden. Does it enrich our senses and our ability to wonder? Does it magnetize our awareness through its compelling beauty? Does it destroy our story line, our sense of self and isolation? Is there a proper balance of Heaven, Earth, and Man? How are the five elements organized and how do they balance? Are all design elements seamlessly integrated making the garden something far greater than its parts? Are intrusive views mitigated? Does the garden satisfy all functional requirements? How does the garden relate to its physical environment? Is it sustainable? How does it fit the cultural and social environment?

Designing a complex garden system, a garden mandala, is a reiterative process, not a linear one. Language forces us to describe the principles and the process in a linear way, but the model is circular and adaptive. The process of design and construction will inform these principles just as the principles inform the design and the construction. Every thought, every action, every external and internal change informs the whole and alters it. The garden is alive, growing and changing, constantly adapting to changes, and so is the process of designing and creating a garden. The garden is not a product but a process.

Step by step we use the View to evaluate the merits and deficiencies of the design. Then we begin the entire process again, using the information gathered from the evaluation to further inform our design process. We begin with meditation, contacting the unborn, limitless realm, and then move to contemplation and visualization. We wait, allowing the reimagined garden image to appear. Once it shows its face, we stabilize it in our mind's eye and look at it closely. We then draw our vision on paper and refine the model accordingly. At that point, the whole thing is ready for a second evaluation. This process should go on as long as necessary until there is agreement among all parties involved that the design has real merit and should be built accordingly.

It is vital that everyone agree on the final design. Often there are quiet parties who go along with the vision but secretly have misgivings about it. Invariably these objections surface at the most inopportune times and can undermine a project. All parties should be actively involved in the envisioning and evaluation process.

I am a big believer in a slow design process where everything is thought through and everyone is in agreement, followed by a swift and unsurprising construction phase. This may seem costly since so much time is spent on planning with nothing actually happening, but it usually reduces the overall cost. It also gives us time to understand the full implications of the design and, if necessary, make allowances for some of the consequences, such as noise, dust, and other disruptions to the environment.

A garden either gets better or it gets worse. So it is with design. The measures of quality are the design's congruency, balance, harmony, and adaptability. Often this is attained through relentless removal of the clutter revealing the simplest, most elegant environment.

OPENING
THE EYES
OF THE
GARDEN

Beauty is spirit, fugitive in matter.
—Plotinus

When the design is complete, we bring the garden into existence. Like a painter "opens the eyes" of the Buddha portrait by painting in the irises, the designer must turn from the intellectual to the practical. This is the nitty-gritty of garden construction and how we build the garden. How can Heaven be victorious over budget engineering?

In constructing the garden, everyone involved will have to understand the vision. This is again where clarity becomes critical. People work better in a team when they can see where the effort is heading. What is the mind we bring to this process? How do we best work with others, our materials, and our responsibilities?

After the birth of the garden comes growth, diseases, and challenges of all sorts. So the spirit of the garden is entrusted to the garden's caretaker. He, perhaps more than even the designer and the garden builder, shapes and becomes the garden. He is in charge of the continuity of the spirit.

MOVE FROM MEDITATION TO ACTION

This is where the rubber meets the road, where the design vision translates into rock, soil, water, cement, electrical conduits, irrigation lines, drainage pipes—in short, the material world. The garden you've planned now goes through the hands of contractors, supervisors, workmen, suppliers, and artisans. It will be scrutinized and evaluated by clients, architects, engineers, and neighbors. It will meet unexpected weather, surprises in site conditions, and the mysterious alchemy of the interaction of its parts, each of which may demand something new of the vision. The garden's designer is responsible for the original vision but also has to allow it to change organically, responding to new information.

This is what Chögyam Trungpa Rinpoche calls "meditation in action," and it applies equally to constructing a garden and to building our lives. We have to learn the same lessons to bring our design into the reality of daily life. We learn to develop self-confidence, maintain our positive motivation, cultivate patience, and become open, flexible, and less self-centered. We learn how to face and work with our fear. We train in cultivating a will for awareness.

Developing self-confidence is key to working with others in garden construction. If the designer doesn't have full confidence in herself, no one else will either. Shantideva, the eighth-century scholar, called self-confidence one of the four supports of all spiritual practice. So whether you're a garden designer or a salesperson or a veterinary technician, you learn to develop confidence in your vision and your abilities.

Almost everyone has a sensitive bullshit meter. After a few words and a minute of body language, people decide whether or not to trust the person in front of them. So in penetrating the fog of "how it's always been done" and "I don't think it will work that way" attitudes, the designer has to trust herself, her vision, and her motivation and cultivate patience.

First, the designer has to have complete trust in who he is and what he is doing. Confidence is not arrogance, which is the posturing of ego. Arrogance has no basis in actual competence, knowledge, or understanding, whereas confidence comes from all three of these things. People with absolute confidence generate trust. Trust is necessary to establish in the beginning and throughout the project. Self-confident designers trust themselves and their visions.

Confidence requires training. It comes from relating to things as they are rather than the way we think they are. We can learn to distinguish between the two through meditation, where we discover the way our fears turn into habits of thought and behavior. We learn how we distort our perceptions and create a version of the world that isn't there. This awareness is like a brightness that illuminates dark spaces. Once these dark spaces have nowhere to hide, they stop being so threatening, and they can no longer undermine our confidence.

Confidence comes from proper motivation and dedication to truth, which we also discover in meditation. The vital truth is what is happening right now, in the present moment; it can't be anywhere else. The garden creator becomes trustworthy when her confidence is rooted in the way things really exist, not in the manufactured way we think they are.

A self-confident person can admit mistakes and take responsibility for things that go wrong. She is present with what is happening, both good and bad, without clinging to her own ego and what will protect her sense of herself. The Tibetans call this *wang thang*, or "field of power." With this kind of presence, the designer can take errors in stride and make herself responsible for things that go wrong even if they are not her fault. The great Buddhist master Atisha spoke to this issue with his statement: "Drive all blames into one." The idea is that rather than looking around to cast blame when errors occur, we should look into our own contributions to the error first and foremost. We take responsibility for everything (after all, everything is a projection of mind). This takes the wind out of the blame game and helps everyone to move forward harmoniously both in fixing problems and in working together as a team.

Second, our motivation should be clear and altruistic. We are not building monuments to our own egos; we are trying to create sacred spaces. This clarity of motivation will help our actions to be free of fear and allow us to act kindly and completely. We have nothing to gain or to hide. The practice of being open and transparent involves being genuine, upright, integrated, and congruent. This enables the designer to relate thoroughly to the person in front of her and not to her idea of who that person is or her expectations of how they ought to be. Although this is our natural condition, it takes many years of training to find power in vulnerability.

Third, we learn how to be patient. Patience is one of the six "perfections" that Buddhists practice. It is not simply holding one's temper or suppressing anger, but a true understanding of the interrelationship between oneself and others. If in developing confidence we have been able to drop our egos and listen to other people, this is a good first step. The next step is to understand the underlying connection of motivation between ourselves and others. If we are all trying to build the best space possible (within a budget), then we have to work together. No one can wave a wand and make the garden appear; it takes the efforts of a lot of people. So we have no choice but to work with each other. This awareness of the fact that we are not creating anything on our own applies to all work. Even the graphic artist who works alone at his computer has to rely on the people who designed his programs and built the hardware, and has to produce something that works with the slogan thought up by another person and connects with the theme that the art is trying to convey. There are always bosses, clients, coworkers, and subordinates who all have to communicate and cooperate in order to accomplish anything.

When, as an owner or designer, we think one of the participants in the project is causing trouble through laziness or misguided motivation, we should remember that this person is impelled by his or her own desires and concerns. We don't get angry at the person just because this is true. Shantideva once asked: If someone hits you with a stick, do you get mad at the stick? In the same way, if someone is led to bad actions, we blame the wrong motivations that drive them, not the individual who is causing the problem because of those faults. That's not to say that we don't deal with the issue; it just means that we do so with clarity and compassion, not anger.

Self-confidence, positive motivation, and patience are all tools for life as well as for work in the garden. I have found that the more I understand who I am, the better the landscape is, and the better my life is.

SHARE THE VISION

Once the designer has established trust through self-confidence, proper motivation, and patience, she shares the vision of the garden. The garden is an adaptive system in which things will change even as the design is realized in the material world. The design is not static and will adapt with the surprises that the site will offer and the unexpected way in which the elements will affect each other as they are installed.

Skilled craftsmen usually have established work habits and are used to doing things in a certain way. It can be difficult for them to be open to different methods and approaches. For example, most crane operators lift known, balanced weights with geometrical, regular shapes, such as bundles of steel bars. They are not used to lifting rocks, whose weight is unevenly distributed and whose center of gravity is not obvious. Rocks can slip from their rigging and be very dangerous for both the crew and the crane operator. It can be done safely, but the crane operator involved has to be willing to learn to work with new materials and to accept new ideas about how to lift loads. This means he will work best if he can understand the inspiration and vision of the garden. Many times I've relied on the perspective of the crane operator for advice on setting stones.

Adjustment of the plans to the larger vision happens on every level of construction. Most contractors are used to following plans that can be precisely specified and that don't change. Yet the first stone set influences the second, and patterns unfold from there. Established grades sometimes have to be adjusted to accord with the rocks set, which affects the pond and how the river flows, which changes the spacing and area available for planting.

The only way I've found to make these adjustments correctly is to establish a common vision for the garden. I don't mean simply communicating an understanding; I mean that each person involved should understand the overarching meaning and aim of the design for the space. It is best to explain the vision in terms of what the garden will be like in the future. For example, the designer might describe the garden as follows: "A visitor will enter the garden through a small structure named the 'Chamber of Gathering Energy.' This is a covered space protected by a large stone arrangement. Next is the path to the main garden . . ."

Plans are great for keeping us all on track, and complex and/or large sites require following the plans carefully. But there also has to be a time for considered changes when surprises occur.

I was once directing a crew of three Israeli and five Mexican men. English was our only common language. We had built a twenty-eight-foot-high mountain out of dirt and large boulders and in the center of the mountain we installed a large concrete box. Then we started shaping a giant mound in front of the opening of the mountain to the inner chamber. I tried to work with each member of the crew to help them understand what I wanted them to do and to encourage them. Still the work went slowly and required constant correction.

One day I gathered them all together and told them that the mountain we had created represented the center of the universe and the chamber inside was intended for the god that created the universe and the protection of his female attendants. (This is taken from one of the Greek myths about Zeus. He was born in a cave and nurtured by female fairies—the naiads—until he was strong enough to take his place as the head of the gods.) I explained that we were shaping that giant mound into the back of a dragon that would protect the cave. It took a few minutes before they caught on and understood. When we returned to work ideas started flowing from everyone about the way to create the best possible dragon. When their creativity was unleashed everyone worked as a team, and the job was done faster and better than it would otherwise have been because we shared a common vision. Everyone left some of themselves behind when we all said good-bye to the garden we had co-created.

This is an example of how effective metaphor can be in describing a vision. We can each understand this metaphor in our own way and even though my reality may not be exactly the same as anyone else's, we can easily communicate to reach an optimal result.

If we are designing our own garden, we should understand our own vision for it. But if we're designing for others, we have to take their views and concerns into account. Though clients are usually involved in the design process of their garden, some get involved in the construction as well. This can be helpful or harmful, depending on the client and our own response to them. We have to communicate our vision to the client and have them find their own meaning in it, before construction starts. When obstacles arise or new ideas evolve, we can deal with them more easily when there is a strong commitment to the underlying vision. When designer and owner are not of like mind for this vision, trouble can ensue.

Once I spent three years working on a design for gardens that would surround an extraordinarily beautiful and magical temple. I worked with the monk in charge of the landscape, and we connected on a level

I've never experienced with a client. He understood my visions perfectly and usually added bold and wonderful ideas.

What I didn't know was that the political system of the monastery was a "consentocracy." All big decisions were made collectively and everyone in the community had to agree to them. The head monk had the power to veto group decisions, but in the history of this monastery that had never been done.

After a lengthy design process for what was to be a garden worthy of the temple, the community decided that the whole project would be disruptive to their contemplative lives. So even after the major excavation had been completed, thousands of yards of soil had been moved, dozens of large boulders (some as large as twenty tons) had been delivered, and suitable machinery had been brought to the site, the project was cancelled.

Although the vision of the garden was perfectly understood by the head monk and me, and scale models were built showing intricate detail so others could clearly see where we were headed, the community did not grasp the vision. They were not properly invited into the vision and never made it their own. As a result, this garden was never built as designed.

The person who designs the garden is responsible for transmitting their vision to other people who likely all see the world in very different ways. This means we find a way to be in deep rapport with people, one by one, who present themselves at all levels of the project, from funding sources to mortar mixers. We all have a conviction that our version of the world is, if not the only true version, then at least the most-true version. We have to remember this when working with others. The beliefs people have about how the world is and works are influenced by factors such as their experience, their society, their profession, their family, their ethnicity, and their race. We add on to that our personal experiences, traumas, fears, anxieties, and neuroses, which are further filters through which we view the world. To work together, we should understand as much about those filters and worldviews as we can, and respect them.

The designer or owner should also be open to the creative suggestions of the team, since we, too, are wearing our own rose-colored glasses when we view the world and our designs. It is important to remember that we all have much more in common than it might appear. In building the garden, we all care about the quality of our work, our authenticity, and our contribution. Our basic nature is caring. When we can direct that caring toward a shared vision, we feel a belonging to something that is greater than we are.

This formula is one we can apply to interactions with all the other people in our lives—the people who share our work space, our car pool, or our home. Listening carefully, understanding the filters we and others have for viewing the world, and respecting and incorporating different points of view or approaches into our projects are all skills we can incorporate into every part of our lives.

BUILD A STRONG FOUNDATION

Once the common vision is established, we can begin building the garden. We start by carefully considering its unseen portions, those things that are vital to the ongoing functionality and well-being of the garden, but are often buried or hidden from view—the drainage, the electrical lines, the irrigation pipes, and so on. This includes foundations, soil modifications, and shaping the terrain.

This is the time when our first surprises can occur. The contractor should have had the utilities located so that the construction won't interfere with electric, gas, or water lines. Soil sampling in advance ensures that the plans will make provision for where and how soil will have to be amended or the plant selection changed in order for plants to grow properly. But the land is filled with surprises, and things happen on-site that we can't anticipate.

When I was first starting my construction business, a client asked me to build a fence along his property line, with posts set exactly six feet apart. Inevitably, partway through construction we found a giant underground boulder exactly where one of the posts had to go. I asked if we could set the post a little farther away from the last one, but the client insisted on the regularity of the post separation. The boulder was too big to dig out of the ground, so we ended up drilling a hole into the rock in order to set that post exactly as requested. This taught me to expect these kinds of surprises and to prepare for them.

How we deal with unexpected conditions and events has everything to do with how strong our vision for the garden is. If we know what the feeling and atmosphere of the garden should be, we can make decisions based on those criteria rather than solving problems based on convenience or momentary impulse. No matter what the obstacle— an unseen rock, an unanticipated site condition, a sudden cut in the budget—we can adjust calmly and still achieve the vision, if not the specifics, of the design.

This is true for every facet of our lives. If we meet the unexpected with dismay and disarray, our lives will constantly be buffeted by the inevitable vicissitudes of chance. We will be at the mercy of our emotions and the whims of others, rather than calmly following a path that we've thought through carefully and which allows for detours and different routes. Meditation practice, based on our life vision, is the means by which we can avoid being blown off course, away from our original intent.

Design is the practice of setting vision. Meditation stabilizes the mind so the designer can focus without distraction on the process. This is an ability we all have and can develop. We first build a strong foundation with study and rumination. From this solid foundation, garden design progresses rapidly. This is the grading and preparation of the mind.

FACE YOUR FEAR

At the beginning, we also deal with our fear. It is terrifying to watch the first rock being lifted into place as the entire crew, the owner, and various people passing by look on. We want to get it right. Everyone has this fear of failure; it's part of doing any kind of work in the world. It arises whenever we have to match a vision or an ideal to a material reality, when we have to put plans into action. Suddenly we are onstage. Our knees wobble. With this fear can come self-doubt.

We react to self-doubt in several ways. One is to become highly analytical, to consider and try to prevent all the things that might go wrong. When this happens in rock setting, you are tempted to measure the rock, weigh it, get engineering advice, and do everything you can think of to make sure things go well. These are not bad preparations, but they are counterproductive when carried too far. At some point the rock has to be set, and no amount of thinking is going to make that happen.

Another common reaction to fear and self-doubt is to become highly emotional, to get angry at coworkers and snap at people who work for you. Any small thing that goes wrong becomes the basis for a blame game in which we try to avoid responsibility and get others in trouble. We might delay the construction or pick a fight with someone on the crew, anything that puts off the time we have to stand up and do the work. Again, this is not a helpful reaction.

When I see myself beginning to be overly intellectual or overly emotional, I recognize that I am not coping well with the fear of turning the ideal into the real. I take a couple of deep breaths and acknowledge to myself that I am feeling this fear. I find where it is in my body—usually the stomach in my case—and I consciously try to fully experience and then relax that part. Then I jump directly into the fear and act.

It is also helpful to remember our motivation for the project and the meaning of the work. It helps to see ourselves as contributing to something much larger than ourselves. It gives meaning to our life and our work.

Fear is simply an empty thought. So why does it grab us by the scruff of our necks and push us around? We should plant our feet on the ground and take our stand. As I said earlier, we can see a thought for the ephemeral thing that it is, without substance and without power unless we give it those qualities. When you face fear, when you don't run away, you can transform its energy into beauty—and then the rocks will sit properly.

LEARN TO LISTEN CAREFULLY

Rock setting is the core of establishing the structure of the garden. With rock setting we place the bones of the garden, and the bones form the skeleton from which the rest of the body of the garden takes shape. We regard rock as the bones of the Buddha. If our aspiration is to create a sacred space, then we regard the rock that animates the space as sacred. We don't relate to it as a material object that can be pushed around, grabbed by the claw of an excavator, or manipulated to fulfill our architectural dream. We treat it with utmost respect. We ask rock to help us to know where it wants to go. Then we assist it to relax and rest comfortably. The rock will sit where it is more or less exactly as we place it for thousands of years.

It may sound strange for me to say that we should listen to the rock tell us how it wants to be placed. Yet trying to force a boulder to sit in a way that it just doesn't want to be will always be difficult and counter-productive. I once tried to set a boulder into a hillside in a manner that I'd planned for some time, taking into account both the size and shape of the boulder as well as its relation to the others in the garden. With the crane operator, the construction supervisor, and numerous crew trying to help, this rock would just not sit correctly. After several tries, I had the crane operator lift the rock above the site again and quieted my mind. Everyone else relaxed for a moment, stepping back and taking a breather. Suddenly, at nearly the same moment, the supervisor and I both exclaimed: "It should go the other way around!" We both saw that the rock would sit happily if we reversed it. And so it did. It occupied the space I had for it on the plan but in a very different way, and that changed everything.

Once I set some boulders along an entry walkway exactly as I had envisioned them in my plan. For some reason I felt uneasy during the whole process, though I couldn't put my finger on what was wrong. That night, I had a dream in which those rocks lifted themselves from the ground and rearranged themselves in a more animated pattern. The next day I had the crew do the same rearrangement, and everything seemed right. Thank goodness for an understanding homeowner, who was also very pleased with the outcome. I had once again learned the lesson to listen to the inner voice and to the wishes of the rock rather than slavishly following a plan on paper.

Listening carefully to what's going on is a life skill that not enough of us learn well. We put a high value on our individual initiative and opinions, sometimes at the expense of listening to hear what the consequences of our actions will be. What's called "deep listening" is not just a matter of being silent while others talk. It requires that we recognize our ego shouting loudly internally, and quiet it. In meditation, we learn to recognize this insistent voice as it tries to distract us, so when it comes up again in conversation, we can calmly ignore it. Once we pacify ego, we find that our ability to empathize with another point of view grows. This is also part of deep listening, a genuine concern with the people and things outside yourself.

LEARN THE ART OF PLACEMENT

As you work in the garden to arrange all its materials according to the way they are shown on your plan, you are continually relying on your perception of balance and straightness. For some things, such as a fence line or a poured pool, you will certainly have to use tools to ensure that your lines are straight and exactly as long as planned. For other things, however, you will have to learn to trust yourself and your inner sense of what looks right. When we do this, we discover how much of what we perceive as "correct" is really a matter of perspective, of how we choose to look at things.

For example, I was taught by one of my Zen teachers, Kobun Roshi, to practice "offering the incense straight." Have you ever tried to place a long stick of Japanese incense—which is very thin—in a bed of ash? See how many adjustments you have to make to get it straight. Look at it from above and from the front and from each side. An adjustment in one direction often throws off another view's straightness. Eventually I would get it perfectly set, only to discover an hour later that though the air was still, the ash had fallen far away from center. What I thought was straight was really not even close.

This practice of trying to find "straight" on a small scale has helped me with planting trees or setting a rock or one of many other things that rely on what it means to be vertical.

This is called the "art of placement." I practice on many things during the day, like placing a broom handle against a wall, placing a candle in its holder, checking my posture and how it is placed in space.

One key to getting something "straight" is to look at it from every possible angle. You learn how the perception of the vertical or the horizontal can be affected by surroundings. For example, it's much more difficult to set a rock straight and vertical when it is on a hill than it is on flat ground.

Neuroscience demonstrates that we are hardwired to see vertical, horizontal, 30, 45, and 60 degrees. All other angles are interpolated. The practice of finding verticality in our bodies and in our placements of objects like rocks and trees is the key to all design arts.

DEFINE THE RELATIONSHIPS WITHIN THE SPACE

When a thing is placed in a defined space, it relates to the boundaries and defines the space. The placement of a second item also relates to the edges, but to the first thing as well, and so forth. The art of placement emphasizes both the inherent quality of each thing as well as the synchronicity between them all. The garden may have many sections and unfold like a novel, with each section celebrating the union of Heaven and Earth and expressing itself in its own way. Each living garden element relates to the space it is in and to its placement in its family, in its community, and its environment. In a garden everything has its place, its orientation, its growth habits, its color and size, and its relationships. At the same time, and equally important, each flower is unique and gives all its life force to be the beautiful individual it is. This is also true of each boulder and each tree.

Another important aspect of placement is to see the scene you are creating as a whole, with relaxed eyes. Rather than focusing exclusively on the tree you are planting or the way a rock fits into the ground, keep your mind vast and your sight on what is around those elements as well. In order to do this, I close my eyes and intentionally relax all of the ocular muscles. Then I open my eyes about halfway and relax into what appears. This makes it much easier to find straight or level or even.

As with any activity, you look for the proper balance between close attention to what you're doing and a relaxed and open mind. We can practice this balance when we're meditating. Too much tense focus on our object (like the breath) will result in joyless exhaustion. Too loose a focus, and we miss something, fall asleep, or our minds wander. The Tibetans compare this to riding a young horse: we have to keep the horse under control, but not grasp the reins too tightly or we risk stopping altogether.

Since the rocks and the shape of the earth element are the first things created in the garden, all other elements will start in relationship to the earth. If care is taken in the rock setting, the rest of the garden unfolds naturally. Waterways, pathways, and plant colonies animate the rock forms and bring the entire composition to life, to vitality, to harmony and balance, to now. But each of these other elements responds to the way the earth element has been formed and the rocks have been set. This may require changes to the plan as the garden is built.

For example, once the mountains and boulders have been set, what was originally designed to be a ten-foot waterfall may now only want to be an eight-foot fall. This in turn changes the second fall, and the subsequent falls and watercourse. And this change creates ramifications throughout the design—the trees will be smaller, the paths may interact differently with the other elements. In responding to the shapes of the land and the bones (rocks) of the garden, the space may have to be made quieter or louder, calmer or more energetic. We allow new information and change to further develop the design vision.

Understanding the way that things relate to each other, both in space and character, is a part of any kind of design work, whether it's architecture, interior design, or even product design. Clarity about our physical and emotional relationships is also part of living a balanced and harmonious life. If we see how a person has similar or opposite qualities to our own, and how that person operates in the world, we can better place ourselves in harmonious relationship to that person, or even choose not to engage with them at all. And relationships change over time. Just as a tree grows and has to be trimmed to maintain the garden's scale, so too may our responses to our environment and the people in it have to change. In order to find the flexibility to recognize and adjust either the garden plan or our life circumstances, we continually return to our meditation practice to keep our minds open and to see every day with fresh eyes.

———————

LEAVE YOUR ATTACHMENTS BEHIND

We have to leave the garden in the beginning, in the middle, and in the end. In the beginning of the design process, we have to drop all preconceptions. All expectations and emotional pressures should be left behind. What has worked in the past, what others have done, we leave behind. Our reasoning, investigation, analysis, envisioning—we leave it all behind. This is the first leaving.

In the second leaving, the garden designer lets go of all attachments to the design. Attachment clouds clear vision and obstructs correct judgment. We sustain a very clear vision of the underlying poetry and communicate that as clearly as possible in a way the listener can understand and listen deeply to whomever is in front of us. We learn to be flexible and quick to adjust to unexpected obstacles, to deviate from the plan when we have to sacrifice some detail in order to accomplish the larger goal.

Finally, after a carefully evaluated and revised design is approved and the garden is built by a contractor, subcontractors, and their crews, the garden designer will turn everything over to the gardener who will maintain it, whether that's the homeowner or a professional. At this point, there has to be a clear and adaptive vision to pass along, expressible in words and images. This is the documentation that will remain the same throughout the evolution of the garden. It will be the reference point for generations.

We encourage a "vision statement," a short written description of the design intent and overall purpose, which could be attached to the physical plans for the garden. This could include the name of the garden, its poetry and intent, and perhaps some specifics about how that intent is to be implemented. It could also include a walk-through of the design, describing everything from the entry experience, the intended overall structure, the borrowed scenery, and other general ideas. It could even get specific on details, explaining how certain rock arrangements should be built or what color the border area should be. If a tree is installed near a rock in order to emphasize the height of the rock, the statement might explain the proportion desired between these two elements. It could describe the intended watercourse of a river in terms of the metaphor it is intended to create. These are all means of continuing the intention of the design into its manifestation.

There is an old saying that "a garden either gets better or it gets worse." Even when we walk away from a newly built landscape, its elements have already begun to grow, die, and change. Sometimes plants don't do well where they are situated, or some natural condition kills them off. They might grow out of proportion and require trimming. All these changes should be made with the overall vision in mind or soon the garden will lose its character and its power. Scale has to be religiously maintained. Of course, the best situation is if the garden designer and the gardener can have some time together so there can be a meeting of minds.

There is some debate about whether the underlying poetry of the garden should be revealed to anyone outside the design team. Does describing a metaphorical relationship among certain elements of the garden cement that single way of viewing into the garden? I think that if there is a strong sense of structure, whether arising from metaphorical arrangements or mathematical proportions, anyone can view the garden and experience its underlying power, balance, and harmony. So getting too specific in the vision statement might foreclose the opportunity for someone to see something else in the design that might be more immediately relatable for them.

If we say that the design is intended to echo a certain Japanese character that has a deep meaning for the designer, does that preclude others from seeing something different? It may, but people are always going to search for the pattern and meaning that are closest to their own hearts and minds. Having a meaningful experience has as much to do with the meaning we bring to the experience as it does with the space itself. I have had clients change the name I gave to their gardens, and often this is delightful evidence that they have made their own profound connection with the space that we have created together.

In transmitting vision, a garden designer is like a calligrapher, offering only what is necessary. The Zen master Kobun Roshi gave me one of his calligraphies for a long retreat. It translated as "one sun." In the character for the sun, I saw the heat of the sun, the majesty of the sun, the meaning of the sun. Every day I awoke and sat with this calligraphy. There was just enough information in the form and the strokes to allow my imagination to fill in richer stories every day.

This is common to all good design. Our tendency is to put in too much when we describe our vision; we should put in only what is necessary to stimulate the imagination of the caretaker. It is much the same as when the imagination fills in a picture that is only outlined, bringing life to the image. On the other hand, a filled-in image allows us no scope to bring it to life. Meaning comes when our imagination fills in a personal picture within a carefully done outline.

As the garden designer leaves the garden for the last time, he bows. The garden is now in the hands of others.

SPACIOUSNESS
AND NOT
KNOWING

Emperor Wu of Liang asked the great master Bodhidharma, "What is the highest meaning of the holy
truths?"

Bodhidharma said, "Empty, without holiness."

The Emperor said, "Who is facing me?"

Bodhidharma replied, "I don't know."

—from *The Blue Cliff Record*, translated by Thomas Cleary

A great Zen Buddhist sage named Dogen Zenji said that we should conform very closely to the cosmic order in all our life's endeavors. The most complete method of aligning with the cosmos is residing in the "don't-know mind." This mind is one in which the ego recedes, where the distinctions between self and other dissolve. It is completely free of expectation, grasping, projections, and iterative thought.

We experience this mind when we practice meditation, and by designing, building, and maintaining the garden from this state, we reinforce and strengthen the don't-know mind so we can carry it into the rest of our lives. We also make it possible for others who enter the garden to experience the same thing. Once we have uncovered this state of mind, we can use it to delve into the unions of opposites that make up the garden.

EXPLORE THE DON'T-KNOW MIND

Don't-know mind is the mind-set of a Buddha—it is when complete openness occurs. The Buddha can maintain this mind all the time; the rest of us aspire to it, but we have what seem like endless challenges to experiencing it. Despite the difficulty in achieving don't-know mind, I believe that nearly all of us, at some time in our lives, have had an encounter with this mind. It is at first experienced as a gap in an otherwise relentless flow of thoughts and projections, a ray of sunlight breaking through a rainforest canopy. It often appears after a life-changing event that forces us out of our complacency. Some people report feeling it when their child is born; some feel it in a quiet moment beside a forest stream; others are in it when they fall in love.

The don't-know mind is emotionally as well as mentally open. It is what connects us to each other at a heart level. When we have expectations of others based on our egocentric minds, we are disappointed and even angry. If instead we approach others with a don't-know mind, we are allowing other people to be as they are and can feel compassion and ease with them.

Experiencing these brief moments at all is a lot more important than their duration. In them, we can clearly see that the nature of don't-know mind is within us and available to us all the time. Knowing this, we can ask ourselves, What stops us from sustaining the don't-know mind? What thought patterns interrupt our listening for it? I find that persistent negative thoughts (pride, jealousy, fear, anger, judgment of both self and others) are major barriers to experiencing this mind. Until we can transform these obstacles, we'll be unable to sustain don't-know mind.

Working with these obstacles begins with awareness. As we've learned, we first have to become completely aware of existing conditions and patterns in our minds and in the environment before we can do anything about them. In meditation, as we look into our own thoughts as they float by, we notice that they create emotional attachments that seem to control the show, even though they are as evanescent as clouds. Like all thoughts, they arise and pass away. Yet we allow them to leave lasting traces by holding on to them as if they are the real thing, as if they are the way things actually are. Once we can see and accept these patterns for the passing phenomena they are, we can learn to let them go rather than allowing them to take over our lives. Awareness of the patterns and how they operate in detail is the beginning of transformation.

If we are going to design a contemplative garden, we have to begin with don't-know mind and let ideas flow from it. Because this state is open and choiceless, it allows us to embrace apparent opposites and encompass them all within the scope of the design.

———————

JOIN CRAFT AND ART

As garden designers we learn a lot of craft. A homeowner designing her own garden will have to know at least a minimal amount of technical information about drainage, retaining walls, plant growth habits, and the like. That kind of knowledge is expected of professional designers and of the construction crews who build the garden. But from the very beginning, when the time comes to put pen to paper (or stylus to screen or backhoe to dirt), this craft should be incorporated into the art of design. What exactly is the "art" of design? And where does it come from?

Freud believed that the sublimation of our basic instincts was the drive that created all art, science, and culture. His view was rooted in the idea that the self was a separate, independent thing apart from and reacting to real outer phenomena over which it had no control. This dualistic thinking led to the idea that art was a thing created from internal impulses that we turned outward in order to create an object that might reflect or communicate the sense of those impulses.

Chögyam Trungpa discusses this ego-driven art in his book, *True Perception: The Path of Dharma Art*. He states that art emanating from our ego is a "tendency to split the artist from the audience and then try to send a message from one to the other. When this happens, art becomes exhibitionism." He suggests the alternative view that art, or design, is created from a certain meditative state of mind that is open and clear and definitely not a projection of the ego.

This kind of art, which Chögyam Trungpa called "dharma art," we might also call art based on meditation. It is a means of seeing and depicting experience with open eyes and no focus on the self. It doesn't have to be pretty or extraordinary or conventionally nice, since our lives encompass the sad, the dark, and the angry as well as the gentle and pleasing. Instead its defining feature is that it springs from a mind that is open, calm, and free of preconceptions. It is based on awareness, not judgment, and it is the product of a human mind that is racing toward reality, not a manufactured sentiment or display of its own brilliance. The inspiration for this kind of art or design is what is before us in the world. It can be everyday experience, it can be nature, or it can be the site for the garden.

This kind of design requires training, as does any discipline. But the training is both in craft *and* in disciplining the mind, and in bringing the two together seamlessly. We can spend many hours learning the names and growth habits of plants and the mechanics of making a waterfall and how to use our CAD design programs. But we should spend an equal number of hours in learning to meditate, in becoming familiar with our own minds. We should be willing to revisit a site or explore a place in nature many times in order to find ourselves truly experiencing it, to be sure that we are not imposing on it our small mind filters.

I have friends who are fantastic horticulturalists. If I show them a photograph of a magnificent waterfall cascading through a mountainside of rock, they will inevitably notice the small white flower to one side, amazed that that particular plant could be growing in such an environment. They bring tremendous attention to detail and knowledge to the garden, but they fail to see it as a whole. Their training has become their filter, and they are looking at a garden without taking in its power and possibilities. As designers, we should be aware of details; they are of course tremendously important. But we can't allow ourselves to become jaded by our craft, by our abilities to walk into a space and know how to deal with it technically. That might make for a successful designer, even a rich one, but it is not going to make for a true design artist, and those spaces will not rise to the level of the exemplary garden. Once we think we know something, we lose our freshness and spontaneity, and we become frozen in place.

Surely this applies to all aspects of our working lives. The expert in any subject is able to see and size up situations efficiently and know what solutions might apply. But if he lacks the kind of *shoshin*, or "beginner's mind" that Suzuki Roshi wrote about, he has cut himself off from real inspiration and the clearest thinking. The trick is to nurture expertise, to learn our craft, without getting away from don't-know mind. That fumbling and clueless mind is also pure and clear, it has no idea what is about to happen. This is where we should pick up the pen to design.

Many people interpret don't-know mind as stupidity or ignorance or incompetence. But in fact it is the open mind that has no preconceptions, that has not made judgments or divided things into categories. It's the design mind that uses a weed as a flower, or a cabbage as a decorative part of a flower bed. It's the mind that sees a boulder as alive and expressive and not just dead rock. It's the ability to innovate, to see each site for what it is and what it can express, rather than deciding what style of landscape suits the architecture.

JOIN TIME AND TIMELESSNESS

The garden connects us with time, in both its linearity and its circularity. It also connects us with the realm of timelessness and infinity. The garden, perhaps more than any other kind of art, can make us aware of time. This is partly because it reveals the cycles of life within time. We can experience the seasons as they pass. We see the garden's processes: seed, germination, growth, flowering, reproduction, and death. Everything and everyone that is born becomes increasingly complex and then dies and is reborn in circular patterns, like the seasons, like everything in the garden.

The garden can also store our memories. In our temple garden, we've celebrated many weddings and funerals. All three of my children were married there. Loved ones and dear friends were honored in their passing. The garden remembers all of these events, and when I am in the garden we share a history. Sometimes the garden commemorates a more ancient history. It might be the site of an extinct civilization or the site of a terrible cruelty we want the garden to acknowledge and transform.

The garden gives us the experience of time as we move within it. We walk along the paths forward and back and look ahead and behind us. There is a certain rhythm to this physical movement. As in music, rhythm locks us in to an experience of time. Rhythm extends into the visual, not merely the kinesthetic. Our eyes move through a composition in a manner determined in part by the design. Almost everyone looks for the source of water, for example, and tracks its course with their eyes. Planting has a rhythm as well, determined largely by the color and size of the plants and their relation to one another.

The materials of the garden can also evoke the sense of time. An old tree, for instance, evokes a past time and connects us with our ancestors. A rock gives a different sense of time from our own, a geological ancientness. A brook is always fresh, never repeating. A flower blooms but is temporary, giving us a sense of the bittersweet passage of time. A waterfall shows us time always passing. Even the way we play with light and dark will suggest the passing of time in a day.

The sights and smells of the garden draw us in to time by allowing us to further drop our outer concerns. The dew on the feather grass in the early morning, the smell of a gentle breeze and its touch on our cheeks and noses, the chirping of a few small birds—these bring us into being alive to what we are experiencing. That feeling of being fully alive comes from leaving our chattering mind behind, checking it at the door, so to speak. This mental chatter—worries and fears of all sorts, who we are, who we think we are, what others think of us—we can leave behind at the gate and enter the garden.

The garden marks time vividly because it is different every week, different every day, different every moment. When something happens in the garden, it happens in an environment that is unique to that moment. Of course, this is true of all our experience, but nothing gives us more markers of time than the garden.

As much as the garden marks time, it also holds the possibility of leading us to a sense of timelessness by bringing us into the present moment where there is no time, no "knowing." Since we usually aren't able to leave behind our complete identities at the gate, there are opportunities throughout the garden to drop them. As we enter the garden, we follow an inviting pathway. We notice the sound, or the stillness. We notice the shape of the mountains and valley. Gradually our mind calms, our masks disappear, and our awareness is heightened. Our breathing slows. More and more we become the garden.

This happens because we are completely in the present moment, completely aware of our surroundings. We can be without ideas, without judgments, and our minds become free. The future is not there, the past is over. The garden brings us into the "right now," and the right now includes all history since the beginning of the universe, and it includes all possible futures.

The Zen master Dogen Zenji called this state "being time," when one is not so much outside of time as one with it. Centralizing on the self creates dualistic thought and dualism separates us from "being time" into spatial time. We have the mistaken feeling, "I am here as the moments go by." The garden can draw us out of that dualism into a sense that we are at one with time. We are aware but not distracted, fully alive instead of half-heartedly existing.

It is curious that when we are in time with time, we experience timelessness. The now seems to become infinite in experience, which gives our mind plenty of space. There's a lot of room in the now, a sense of both openness and relaxation. Now becomes outside the limits of time, a completeness that is not harassed by the past or pulled forward by the future.

We have all had strange "out of time" experiences, either at moments of great peace or great happiness or under great duress. Those who have come close to dying often report a life review of all their actions and thoughts from birth through the present time that seems to unroll out of time but completely. This happened to me when I was in my twenties. I contracted malaria in India while serving in the Peace Corps and technically died. In those few moments before I was revived, I could see and judge each of my life's experiences until then.

Even in a less difficult experience, perhaps while rock climbing or sky diving, we can feel so completely absorbed—or frightened!—that time stretches out infinitely and we forget ourselves. One such experience happened to me at Chögyam Trungpa Rinpoche's cremation. His body was placed in a stupa on top of a very large mound of logs. The stupa was surrounded by groups of Tibetan monks chanting, ringing bells, and blowing horns. Many had been there chanting with the body all day and night for several days. The flames grew and grew and the heat was amazing. Smoke billowed upward in thick clouds. Far above the smoke in a blue sky, there appeared a triple circular rainbow. I have never seen a circular rainbow before, let alone a triple one. I was entranced and so completely absorbed in the moment that I completely forgot who I was.

These are the kinds of experiences available to us when we give up our small mind and become completely open. Meditators work for a long time to achieve this complete presence on the cushion. I would argue that we can also find it in the garden.

Though these peak experiences may only occur once, or for only a short span of ordinary time, they can have huge consequences in our lives, especially if we continue to explore their nature in meditation. These openings are opportunities to understand something beyond the veil of the ordinary and to turn the ordinary into insight. Without some framework for understanding these experiences, they may be nothing more than once-felt epiphanies without consequences. If we doubt their reality, or if we realize that there are no words to describe their content, we may never contact them again. Here is where further training with a meditation teacher can lead us on from insight to stabilized realization.

JOIN LIGHT AND DARK

We understand space from the play of light and dark. When there are shadows we understand how the sunlight is angled over the garden. We experience one because of the other. In the same way, we bring our own darkness with us to the garden. We carry our mental and emotional burdens of grief, anger, and pain wherever we go, including places of work, the basketball game, the kitchen, and the garden. After all, the first truth that the Buddha taught is that life is filled with suffering. Undeniably, every one of us faces at least the same three basic causes of pain in life: sickness, old age, and death. We lose our jobs, we part from friends in anger or betrayal, our family members die. All of this is part of the human experience. Even passing joys are part of that suffering, since we can't hold on to them and are pained by their disappearance.

The liberation that can be found in the garden is not the same as just forgetting these difficult aspects of our lives. Instead, when we are in the garden we have the chance to experience them safely and to see how they affect our sense of the sunlight, the positive in our lives. The promise of the garden is not that the pain of living will go away but that it, like the passing of the seasons, will change. The garden can show us that there is something larger than the things that hurt us or make us glad, something beyond these winds that blow us here and there at the whim of circumstances. The garden is not some New Age spaceship that flies us to a pleasurable place where there is no hardship. It offers us something more, and more difficult. It shows us in detail how we divide ourselves from everything around us, how we separate the dark and the light.

In the garden we meet a space that is balanced between light and dark. This balance is not static, but dynamic, a continually changing landscape that nevertheless is always balanced. All the aspects of design that I've spoken about—scale, chiaroscuro, the connections between the path and the waterway—are the tools required to create this balance.

When we enter a garden we feel this balance on a cellular level, not intellectually. Of course a professional designer or an artist might take the time to figure out why a particular composition works so well, but the first impression is not analytical or even emotional. The balance is not a concept, but a felt experience.

Once we have an experience of this kind of balance, our bodies and minds can respond to it and find a place of ease and comfort. We can open to it, which is the first step in liberating ourselves from the imbalance and suffering in our own lives. As the Buddhist saying goes, "Pain is inevitable; suffering is optional."

How is it possible to avoid suffering? One step is to see that the possibility of something beyond suffering exists. There is a condition of being that accepts the pain and grief that we have as humans but also sees them as the play of Heaven and Earth. It is the openness that eliminates divisions and categories—it is don't-know mind. Many people have the mistaken view that a realized being no longer experiences pain but exists in a kind of floating haze of pleasure. But this is not true. There's a story about the Tibetan master Marpa that illustrates this. Marpa was a farmer who was devoted to bringing the pure teachings of Buddhism to Tibet. He spent many years in grueling travel to India, gathering texts and translating them into Tibetan, and bringing them back to his homeland. He became highly realized, yet when his son died, he could not move from his bed, spending days weeping with grief. One of his students was amazed and asked him why—as an adept who had come to understand that all experiences are ultimately part of spaciousness, without true existence from their own side—did he cry? Marpa replied that he was crying because his son had just died.

We are always going to have difficulties as long as we inhabit human bodies. But the garden gives us the chance to find don't-know mind, to go beyond our pain to a place of balance and harmony.

JOIN HEAVEN AND EARTH

Joining Heaven and Earth is not an abstract activity. Both Heaven and Earth have enormous energy, each quite different from the other. So when we join Heaven and Earth, it is not like solving a puzzle or arranging the furniture. We are creating an entire mandala, an entity filled with power and potential. The garden space within the boundary should be a whole. While that might be expressed differently stylistically, the overall feeling of being a complete creation should be there. But what exactly are we joining?

Heaven is the half of the equation that is unchanging and perfect. It is not a place or a thing, but a kind of spaciousness that encompasses all understanding. Heaven is still and strong, but unseen and unknowable through ordinary consciousness.

Earth is what supports us, our basis. And Earth is always changing. With birth, there is death, and everything in between is only around for a tiny fraction of a moment. Earth is continual motion and pliability. We know it through the experience of time and change.

When Heaven meets Earth, it is explosive. It is a dance—a dynamic, evolving, unpredictable, wonderful dance—the ultimate tango. The joining of Heaven and Earth activates them both: Earth is only geology until activated by Heaven; Heaven is unseen until it becomes manifest in Earth.

If the garden truly joins Heaven and Earth, that part of us that has become the garden is also the joining of Heaven and Earth. The experience of the garden can give us a reference point of dynamic balance and have transformative effects on us. These transformations can be small in the beginning, but they can have enormous consequences over time. So I encourage everyone to answer the question, "Who are you and what do you do?" with the answer, "I am a designer." It is an identity worth pursuing. It is inexhaustibly surprising, slippery, and hard to hang on to.

Don't expect too much of yourself in the beginning. Even practicing small parts of garden design will bring benefit. Be content with new beginnings. Every day is a new sun.

Peeking through the Emptiness of Space

A flower doesn't bloom in the sky.
The sky blooms in the flower.

Beware of where you put your mind
A peeking flower may be watching you.

ACKNOWLEDGMENTS

Many years of experience in building gardens have gone into this book. Those gardens would not have been possible without the clients, and we thank those who trusted us to create spaces that are sacred to them and all who visit them.

We began this book on Kauai during our visits there. For their generosity in helping to make those trips possible, we would like to thank Jim and Natalie Levin. Vel and Valle Alahan as well as Dasan were wonderful friends and hosts to us while on the island. Sadasivananda Swami offered his kindness and friendship there as well.

Scott Peppet plowed through an unwieldy and messy first draft and gave us invaluable suggestions. Our editor at Shambhala, Jennifer Urban-Brown, was instrumental in helping the book come together in a coherent whole. We thank both of them for their patience and encouragement.

We are more than grateful to our teachers: Kobun Roshi, Tenzan Keibun Roshi, and Chögyam Trungpa Rinpoche for Martin; Tara Tulku Rinpoche, Gen Lam Rimpa, and Denma Locho Rinpoche for Alxe. True insight comes after connecting to a teacher and a lineage.

APPENDIX 1

A Guided Meditation/Visualization to Open the Space of the Mind before Designing

Begin with a dot.
A dot has no dimension and no time, yet contains all the
    energy of the universe.
Visualize a dot.
Let the dot meet dimension, becoming line. With line
    there is length and direction.

From the center of your line, extend a perpendicular line
    of equal length.
This gives you four directions and two dimensions.
The length of each line is equidistant from the center.
Extend all the lines in all directions simultaneously.
The outline of what you see now is a circle in a flat plane.
This is area.
This was the ancient Greek description of the earth.

From the midpoint, the center, extend an equal line in a
    perpendicular direction to the flat plane.

Now you are visualizing three dimensions: north, south, east, west, up, and down.

This is volume—mounds and crevices, mountains and valleys.

If we extend the original line equally in all directions, we see a sphere.

Now we add time as another dimension.

Can you imagine time as a dimension?

APPENDIX 2

Working with the Five Elements

The five elements are part of an ancient way of naming and classifying the atomic and biological structures of the universe. Always seeking in body, mind, and environment to keep dynamic balance and harmony is the way to good health and happiness. Contemplative design shares the same goals. By understanding the five elements and how they penetrate both the relative and absolute worlds, we understand how much further our designs can integrate with the existing moment. The pieces that follow give more specific detail on working with each element.

Earth

The earth element in the garden is represented by soil and rocks. We start with this because it is the basis for all the other forms of the garden. We begin with a piece of land with existing topography. The very first thing to consider is that there is no reason it must remain in its original condition. As long as we make adequate provisions for proper drainage, we can dig down and build up. We can make ponds and, with the soil we remove (or bring in), we can create mounds, hillocks, escarpments, mountains, slopes, valleys, and all manner of landforms that together make the body of the garden. These forms influence what can be seen from any given point of view. They determine pathways. They establish the basic patterns and relationships in the garden. When the shape is "just right," divine energy takes shape as these mounds. Boulders animate these shapes and their relationships to the other elements of the garden.

Rocks don't grow or change shape. They weather well and are unaffected by the changes of seasons and light. They remain the same when all else changes; they are the stable energetic pattern of the garden.

Rocks give an ancient quality to the garden. Rock relates us to time and gives us perspective on our lives. I personally am convinced that many rocks are conscious. They just have a very different relation to time and space than we do. It is amazing how some not-so-alive rocks can come to life when they are restored to a meaningful relationship with other elements.

When I begin a project, I first estimate how many stones I will use. The number of stones is not arbitrary; it depends on how I believe the stones will establish a resonance with each other and with the structure and the remainder of the space.

Once I have determined the number of stones needed, I roughly decide how many of these will be large, medium, and small. All of these terms are relative to the size of the rocks and the scale of the garden. If the scale requires the large stones to be eight to ten feet in one dimension, then the medium stones might be five to eight feet in one dimension, and the small stones two to five feet. If the large stones are smaller, then the other sizes are selected relative to the size of those stones. It is very important to understand that we are not just making a rockery. We are defining the structure that joins Heaven and Earth. We are forming the body of the garden.

Study each rock and measure its height, width, and breadth. I use a bamboo stick for measuring because the nodes on the bamboo are an easy reference. It is also important to touch the rock and feel its energy. Examine its contours, fractures, and geologic imprints.

Working with stone is a lot different from working with concrete or metal. Rocks can have spirit, though not all seem to. There are live rocks and building blocks. Live rocks are the bones of the garden. Building block rock can be used for walls, edges, shims, foundations, and the like. It is important to distinguish the live rocks from the blocks and ensure that their number corresponds to the intention of the design.

After I have decided how many stones to use and have chosen the stones and sorted them into sizes, I make offerings and calm my mind. Recognizing that what I don't see far exceeds what I do see, and what I don't know far exceeds what I do know, I make offerings to all the spirits present, particularly the spirits of the land. I ask them to protect the site and the safety of all who build, care for, and experience the garden, to grant their blessing and inspire a garden that will bring realization, well-being, and inspiration immediately upon entering through the gate.

This is usually a private ritual, sometimes attended by owners and occasionally by people who will be working on the garden. Once, I was working with a crew of men who showed no outward sign of being interested in anything spiritual. They surprised me, though, when they asked to be part of the ceremony. They brought corn and apples as offerings and stood quietly during the chanting. Every day throughout the project, they started with offerings of corn.

For my part, I promise to create an environment that includes all the known and unknown participants, and I promise that the environment will enhance everyone's life. Finally, I ask for guidance in the setting of the stones and patience with my ignorance. Doing magic takes both mastery and humility.

There are some basic rules in designing rock in the garden. The first stone is called the "ki" stone. This is to energy what the center of gravity is to gravity. It is the center of force in a karate kick or punch. It is the first stroke in a painting, the first move in a game of chess.

Once it is set, the ki stone influences the location and orientation of all other rocks. Each rock sits at a specific distance from and in relation to the ki stone, or a friend of the ki stone's family. If the ki stone is upright and masculine in nature, then the next stone might be horizontal and receptive, a third might unite the first two and circulate the energy between them. All other stones will relate in some way to the ki stone or its primary group.

We can think of stone setting as creating families. The original ki stone might be the head of one family. Another family will have different ki stone, but the original stone influences how it is oriented and where it is located, at what height and in what surroundings.

Stones are arranged in groupings. Each grouping has its own internal organization and all groupings relate to one another. As we have noted before, the mind constantly seeks patterns and similarities. So we sort the stones and then seek order within that sorting.

The simplest and most fundamental rock arrangement consists of three stones, representing Heaven, Earth, and Man. The Heaven stone is upright and perfectly balanced on its vertical axis. The Earth stone is horizontal, receptive. This is the yin and the yang relationship—active/receptive, vertical/horizontal, male/female. The third stone, the Man stone, unites the first two. It provides a vital link by shape, gesture, position, or form.

This relationship between arrangements can be based on metaphors—the Buddhist or Christian trinity; emperor, queen, and child; mountain, water, and sky; and so on. This organization of threes is deeply seated in our consciousness. Three notes make a chord. Three colors (red, yellow, and blue) generate all colors. The triangle with its three sides is the most stable geometric form. Three represents the unity of opposites.

These families of stone have internal relationships. If you are designing rocks in groups greater than three, it's best if you can indicate something about how the rocks will relate to one another in order to guide the builder. The boulders can be organized to form shapes—a crown, a stool, a star, a scepter, a trident, a bow and arrow, or a horse. We might have a five-stone arrangement resembling a mother, father, and three children walking on the beach. Another family of stones may form a cliff at the edge of the beach. A third may form a distant island near the horizon. When we experience the garden, we may not see the shapes but we sense an order. It might not be a mathematical order, but it somehow makes sense to us. It is an energetic, metaphorical order.

Each group of stones relates to all the others and to the whole. Together they constitute a very important part of the poetry of the garden. When stones talk to stones, and groups of stones talk to other groups of stones, the garden comes alive in a way that is magical.

The plan for the garden will show you roughly the size of each rock and where each rock should sit, but the plan can't anticipate or direct the orientation of each rock or its specific scale in the landscape. Before placing it, the builder must decide where the head and the face of the rock are, and at what height the top of the rock will be.

Many people look at a rock and decide that the pointiest end goes up, and the fattest end is the back. But this leads to unimaginative arrangements in which the rock seems awkward. Instead, we should look for the "head" and "face" of the rock first. The head will be the topmost part of the rock and will determine the rock's relationship in scale to other materials, and the face will be the way the rock will be oriented with respect to either the primary viewing area or another rock that will "look at" the first.

A frequent mistake people make in working with rock is to forget the importance of scale on the vertical axis. They might follow textbook style and bury one-third of the base of the rock, with no attention paid to where this positions the head. In order for any rock to correctly match the scale of the grouping it sits in and the other materials surrounding it, it might require burying two-thirds of the rock's base or shimming the rock and building up the soil level beneath it. The top of the rock is critical. The bottom is where the adjustments should be made!

After you have chosen each rock and decided where its head and face are and how it will sit and at what height with respect to the other rocks and to the viewer, the next step is to get the rock from where it is lying to where it is going to live. You must decide on the best equipment and crew to do this. Never grab a boulder with the claws of an excavator or push it around with a bulldozer. This is disrespectful to the rock and your relationship to the rock, and it can damage the rock.

Once you have the rock near to where it will be set, you need the right equipment and crew to set it properly. Since the rock's head needs to be at a very specific height and looking in a certain direction, it is best to lift the rock so that it is suspended from the gravitational center, with the head upright. To do this, you rig the rock with straps or chains or cables and lift it so that when it is in the air it is exactly as you want it to rest when you place it back on the ground. In this way, you can see exactly where you need to dig or shim the base of the rock. Many people push the rock close to where they want it and then bang it this way and that until it suits them. This drives me crazy. Rock setting has to do with identification with the rock itself and shouldn't involve that kind of rough treatment.

Even when choices are carefully made and plans are quite specific, you can have surprises. I built a garden in Los Angeles where the property was shaped like a bowl, dropping from the road over sixty feet. I intended to retain the hillside with large boulders, and to build several falls from the top to the bottom of the garden. In that area, we could only work during certain hours and days. The boulders were coming from far away, and the trucks carrying them could travel by public highways only between certain hours. So our time was extremely precious once the rocks arrived on-site.

I went to the quarry and numbered the 108 rocks I had selected with white marking paint, based on how I was going to set each rock. When I left the quarry I asked them to deliver the rocks in numerical order. They agreed, but before they began delivery, the owner of the quarry threw in a "special gift" for buying so many big rocks: he sandblasted all the rocks to deliver them completely clean. In the process, all the numbers were removed.

At the job site, I had the waterfall excavated and foundations poured for the first seven rocks that I expected. I had photos and sketches of each of my rocks. But none of the ones on the first truck looked anything like the ones I had expected. I called the quarry and was told the sandblasting story. We could get only one truck a day within the road and community restrictions, so I couldn't send this one back. And even if I did, I would have no idea of what boulders were coming next.

The crane was there ready to set rocks, and a large crew was there to dig or fill as necessary, help with the rigging, and more. I had to work with what presented itself. I studied each rock until I felt that we had made some kind of a relationship, and then we set a truckload by the end of the day. I had to repeat this process every day with a surprising new set of rocks delivered in completely random order. Fortunately, I had the vision of the garden clearly in my mind, so each rock and watercourse choice could be made in accordance with that, if not with the original plan.

This means that when setting rock, the builder must always be open and spontaneous, fresh, gentle, and tender but also decisive and confident. One thing for certain is that it will not go exactly as you expect it to go. Rocks never sit exactly as you visualize them. You must respond to the willingness of the rock and from there everything else will change.

The way one rock sits will change the selection of the rock that sits next to it. This is why we spend so much time getting to know the rocks. This has something to do with knowing the size, the head and face, the color, and the nature of the rock, but it also has to do with knowing the spirit of each rock. While knowledge can inform intuition, it is no substitute for it. We must "listen" to the rock.

The way we shape the earth influences how we move through the garden, where we stop, where the water flows and pauses, where we need shade and sunlight, and how we experience space. The shape of the earth hides some views and opens others, shifting as we move visually or physically through the garden. Earth's shape structures what is masculine and what is feminine and the dialog between the two.

Water

When I was a young boy, a respected adult told me that "water purifies itself in its own length, and it is the only thing on earth that can do this." From that day onward I've believed in the magical nature of water. Today, as a Zen monk, I use water as an offering and purification.

Water is in all living beings (people are made up of about 70 percent water) and thus is a great unifying factor between ourselves and the garden. Water's reflectivity is also a great unifier. In the water's surface we see a meld of the mountain form, the trees, the flowers, the sky, and the moon. Everything together is laid out on the water's surface.

When we design with water we need to consider sound, direction, flow, and reflectivity. If we are creating a pond, we have to decide whether we'll have fish and water lilies and whether the water will be clear or cloudy (if the pond has a mud bottom). If the water will be clear, what will the bottom look like? The darker the pool, the more reflective the surface. A black pool is like looking into a mirror. And what is reflected? Principally the sky, the sun, and the moon. How better to join Heaven and Earth?

Next we consider the edge treatment and how the pond will balance with the surrounding environment. We think through where the primary viewing corridors will go and what will be reflected in the pond from each of these points of view.

If the garden will have a river or creek, we determine what course it will take and what sound it will make. Will the sound be bright and gurgling or swishing and flowing? Will it be loud, barely audible, or in between? We also need to analyze the sound from the various stopping places and understand the relation of the sound to the walkways.

Whether designing a pond or a creek, we consider how the use of the water element will affect the rest of the garden. In other words, how will human use impact the garden and how will the garden affect the human use?

Since the garden has boundaries, the flowing water must come from somewhere, follow a course, and end up somewhere—either exiting the garden or flowing into a pool. Too often I see water spouting up from a rock, falling over some other rocks, and ending in a pool, none of which looks natural or beautiful. If we are evoking a natural metaphor it is best to have water imitate natural processes. Clouds gather around mountains and the rain and snowmelt create rivers that flow into valleys. The waterways do not start at the top. Most often I have water emerge from a blind, an obscurity created by a mass of shrubbery, a hidden source. Sometimes I imitate a mountain spring or high alpine pond as the water's source.

The garden designer studies the natural environment in the vicinity of the garden carefully, searching for something that might be important to the design. It is always easier to copy than to invent, so with so much to do, it is best to copy nature if that's possible. Of course, the designer should know how to adapt ideas from nature, often with different rocks and plants and a different background environment, but without losing the quality of the original experience.

I often work in mountainous areas. I study alpine ponds and their settings to plagiarize them. I study narrow mountain falls and the pattern of the boulders that support and direct the water because it helps me create watercourses in the more controlled environment of the garden.

Next we marry the flow of the waterway with the form of the earth. When the grade is steep the water flows quickly and directly, unless it encounters the obstruction of a rock or earth mass. When it levels out the water slows and winds through the meadow.

Water ends up in a pool, a pond, or an estuary. The transition between flowing water and a pond is an opportunity for a waterfall. In Japanese Buddhist mythology, the waterfall is a symbol of the Immovable Wisdom King, the protector of truth. It has a special sacredness, and the sound it makes should be compelling.

Many traditional Japanese garden design texts consider waterfalls to be the most important elements of the garden and give specific instructions on how they should be built. But no matter how we construct it, the waterfall should make sense in the overall context of the garden and its topography. We have all seen too many waterfalls arising from nothing and falling haphazardly into nothing, which would never happen in nature. If you are faced with the situation where a client would like a waterfall but not the mountain it would come from or the pond or river into which it would feed, perhaps it's better to suggest a fountain instead.

We need to understand the feeling of the waterfall. Do we want a single cascade with a high volume of water, a single cascade with a thread of water, a three-part fall, a five-part fall, or a seven-part cascade? We also need to think about which direction each fall will face relative to the viewing corridor and the rest of the garden mandala—it is like setting a sculpture within a mountain.

Again, we should look to the basic principles of design to test our landscape plan. The designer must consider the proportional relationship of the heights, widths, and the lengths of the cascades in a waterfall. Also, where is the waterfall located in the garden mandala? Water amplifies energy when it is still and even more so when it is animated.

So waterfalls should go in power spots, places where auspicious energies gather.

If we have a pool or a pond, its shape is important. In Japanese gardens a pond's shape is often derived from a letter or word or a reference to a poem or a scene from a Noh drama. The most common character, *shin*, means "heart/mind." This particular character, when laid out on the ground, has the quality of concealing some part of the water no matter where the viewer may be. There is always something unseen, something to be discovered.

The pond may be the shape of a crane or a turtle, a lizard, a word, or any symbol. It could be in the shape of a vesica piscis, looking like an eye. We look through our eye at the pond's eye looking at the sky. This is another way of joining Heaven, Earth, and Man.

Water is an important tool to heighten awareness. The sound of a waterfall or a babbling creek always enters into our auditory awareness. It enters and invites. We listen more closely, more attentively. Flowing water has a very definite music. Once the rate of flow is established, we tune our streams by adding many sizes of cobble into the streambed. We can get a bright and lively sound or a deep, cavernous sound and everything in between. Fish and water lilies also help to heighten awareness. Koi, especially, are engaging creatures as well as exquisitely beautiful.

There are always layers of meaning, both obvious and unseen, in any design, including that of water. The pond, to me, represents Buddha nature, our basic clear and luminous mind that is neither created nor destroyed. For other designers, perhaps the pond is the re-creation of the water next to which the designer had an epiphany some years ago.

The crucial quality of water's energy is that it amplifies the energy of its surroundings. If it is in the east, it amplifies the energy of the rising sun. If it is in or near the center, it emphasizes centeredness. Water also moves in a specific, intentional direction, and it moves energy along with it. Even dry watercourses (as in a dry waterfall, dry stream, or dry pond) amplify the energy of their surroundings.

Fire

The fire element of the garden is its plants. Flowers and ground covers are plants of the ground plane, the Earth dimension. Shrubs and small trees comprise the Man dimension. Trees are the overhead element and represent Heaven.

Flower design often focuses too heavily on color. Flowers blossom for only a short while, and most of the time we are left to enjoy the plant itself: its foliage, shape, form, and habits. The shape of the plant and its behavior are primary. Of course, we might tolerate a less than desirable shape for a beautiful flower or a powerful fragrance, as with a lilac or a mock orange. Texture is also important: some plants are spiky like yucca, and some are fuzzy like lamb's ears. Some, like geraniums, are rounded and spreading, and some, as in many hosta varieties, have variegated foliage. We need to pay attention to leaf shape and habit, as well as the overall plant shape. Is it mounding, rounded, triangular, upright, prostrate, or spreading?

We also consider the plant's habits. Does it like sun, shade, or filtered light? Does it like rich or sandy soil, well-drained earth or clay? How much water does it need and how often? Who does it want as neighbors? Plant compatibility is crucial for the sustainability of the garden as well as the harmony it conveys.

Finally, is it a thug or a princess? Some plants want to take over and expand in all directions as quickly as possible. Others are delicate and fragile. Putting these two types together will lead to unhappiness.

When we contemplate our design, we again put on the filtered glasses of Zen design principles. Does the plant design heighten awareness? Usually, this is somewhat automatic. Plants are fully alive and tend to engage us with their beauty, their texture, their color, their interaction, and their fragrance. They are also momentary; some flowers last only one day. The same flower can look quite different in the morning dew than it does in the heat of a summer afternoon. This quality of transience, ephemeral existence, is a constant reminder of the fleeting quality of our own lives and the immediate importance of finding meaning and realization.

The designer needs to use restraint in this world of too many possibilities. The planting plan can easily become busy and instead of heightening awareness can lead to distraction, overload, and mental chatter. We must remind ourselves of the merit of simplicity.

On the other hand, we need enough interest to magnetize our senses and enrich our sensibilities. Subtle, controlled use of contrast helps with this. We can contrast size, form, texture, and/or color. One blue blossom in a field of yellow may be enough.

Proportion and scale are also vital considerations. The importance of a rock arrangement can be negated by a tree out of scale with the rocks. This is a frequent mistake. We often don't control the growth and habits of our trees and shrubs, and as the years go by, their haphazard growth destroys the balance and clarity of the garden. The garden becomes too dense and consequently unhealthy.

Once, I set a large rock with a vertical dimension of sixteen feet in an arrangement. In front of it I planted an alpine fir tree that was three feet tall. The contrast of the small tree and the rock enhanced the experience of the grandeur of the rock. This would continue to be the case if the tree grew to five feet. However, if we let it go, without shaping and trimming, it would crowd the rock, and the rock would lose its dimensionality and majesty.

When we design with trees, we design for either how large they will become or how large we'll allow them to become. If we take the former approach, we may have to wait for many years before the actual balance of the garden manifests. If we start off in perfect balance, we need to carefully control the growth of all the plants, constantly adjusting and adapting them to ever-changing proportional relationships.

When designing the understory plants, the shrubs, I usually think of a shaped mass. These forms interact and communicate with the landforms and the rock settings. We need to consider the height of each mass, its width and breadth, and how it relates in proportion and scale to other shrub masses and landforms.

Flowering plants occupy the ground plane, and we can find pleasing relationships between the areas that the various plants occupy. Perhaps one plant inhabits three square feet, another five square feet, and a third four square feet. This creates the relationship 3:4:5—the Pythagorean triangle and the generator of the golden mean. Another design might have three peonies, four irises, and five poppies, again creating this pleasing proportion.

The order of design is not at all linear, as you might have understood by now. When designing with plants, sometimes I start with flower color and then add the plant form and attributes seeking a balanced composition. Most often, it is a rapid back and forth process.

There are constraints on what we can plant and where. Plants all have specific soil, moisture, and light preferences and are particular about which plants they are happy to have as neighbors and which make them miserable. In almost all cases we find that plants that are happy growing together also look good together. They may not flower with the colors we had in mind, but the colors they exhibit work beautifully, maybe to our surprise.

It is a mistake to design plants from photographs and descriptions. We must know the plants we are using as deeply as we know the land with its contours and nuances. We need to experience the plants from infancy through their maturation and their death. We need to know the inner being of the plant as we experience it. What effect does it have on us? For example, the alpine currant, for me, is calming and forgiving. Its foliage is delicate and its leaves are endlessly interesting. It forgives me when I whack it down to two feet as a mound on a hillock. It is unassuming and yet delightful.

Plants form an intricate web of patterns in the garden. A drift of gaillardia may relate to five other drifts of gaillardia in the garden. Our relentless search for patterns relates these drifts with rhythm and flow. Our eye may move from one mass to another in a flowing, rhythmical way. Or, we may notice the rhythm through the movement of our bodies as we pass from drift to drift. The yellow in the gaillardia may relate as well to a nearby drift of rudbeckia, the yellow color being similar. It may also relate to a red echinacea, the reds of the gaillardia and echinacea somewhat similar.

Patterns created by form, color, or species relate as flow and rhythm as well. Grasses of different species relate to one another, and we find a pattern within them and as our eye moves. They are also beats in the garden's rhythms and lead the eye to flow throughout the matrix of similarities.

The garden design is a dynamic balance of all components. We need to contemplate the balance within the plant design and the relationship of the plants to the landforms, rocks, and water, as well as pathways and structures. Nothing should dominate at the diminution of something else.

Air

The air or wind element in the garden can be found mostly in paths and stopping places. Wind is movement, and paths provide a surface and a direction for motion.

Pathways are of two varieties: straight and meandering. Straight pathways have more yang, or masculine, energy and encourage rapid movement with a sense of destination. Where they end up is all-important. Often they are emphasized with repetition of elements such as columns or trees at regular intervals along the path. Or they have internal rhythm: six steps up to a landing, then six more steps to another landing, and so on.

Meandering pathways are more yin, or feminine, in quality and are most frequently the type used in the garden. As a path curves and meanders, each step reveals a new vignette, perhaps a purple flower just in bloom, or a vista framed by a tree. At the same time, something is lost: the view we just found so compelling is now hidden. Change happens, and it is neither a cause for celebration nor regret. We compose the garden with this in mind so that each step reveals something new and compelling. This brings us constantly back the present moment, back to awareness.

Pathways can ascend and descend as we move through the shaped earth. In the garden, it is best if this happens with level steps. That way the horizontal plane we experience as a level field between the eyes and the ears is uninterrupted and our contemplative feeling is maintained.

Pathways lead to destinations we call stopping places. These can be stones to stand on, benches, decks, and structures. The stopping place sets the point of view from which the landscape is regarded. It is our primary point of reference for composing a balanced and beautiful composition. Composition is based on how the eye travels. What leads our eye and draws our attention? How do we visually move through the garden? Remember we are always looking for patterns and similarities to form into patterns. We look for similar shapes and forms, similar heights, similar colors, similar qualities, and similar proportions and spacing. We sort for scale and contrast and look for patterns there. In the stopping place we want our minds to stop and be quiet and our hearts to open. The rocks should be beautiful in themselves and arranged in a stable and confident way. The trees should be thoughtfully shaped and trimmed, each the appropriate size for its location and elegant in form.

What we are calling stopping places can be as much dwellings for the imagination as they are functional places for occupancy. For me, a hermit's hut, far removed from civilization and lost in the majesty of nature, is a compelling image. I find myself re-creating this longing in my designs whenever I can get away with it.

I am also drawn to the mystery of the cave and the grotto. A German landscape scholar told me that the historical gardens in Germany all contain grottoes. These commemorate the myth of Zeus, who first appeared as a baby in a cave and was nurtured by the naiads, or water nymphs. When he grew up, he created all the forests and gardens of the world for the constant delight of his precious naiads. The grotto is the source of the garden's spirit. Connecting the garden to this mythical foundation expands its depth into the preconscious foundations of human psychology.

From the perspective of the journey along the garden path, we can examine the scale and proportion of all the garden's elements. We can notice how the landforms change as we move. Perhaps three landforms meld into one from one point of view and then slowly open up as we continue. We can study the flow and rhythm of the plants. We can examine whether the garden appears whole, no matter where we are.

Pathways are a moving viewpoint made up of discrete small steps. Here the techniques of conceal and reveal and borrowed scenery play a paramount role. Each step or every few steps should reveal a discrete and yet complete composition. Each picture should have a compelling center of interest (or focus) and a balance of Heaven, Earth, and Man, as well as proper scale and proportion. Composing a path is like breaking time into moments and composing each moment as a discrete entity unified by time.

On the garden path, we can experience intimate environments, taking us to places in time and space far from the moment at hand. We can also catch a glimpse of infinity. In one garden, I built a water basin situated along a path where one could see nothing but the immediately surrounding plants and landforms. It was a constricted, narrowed feeling. The water basin was on the ground, and one had to bend way over to fill the ladle to get a drink or wash one's face and hands. From that position, suddenly there was a view that penetrated well beyond the garden and looked directly at the distant horizon. This must be similar to looking back at planet Earth from a space capsule. Once again we can see how garden design can affect our perceptions and experiences.

One of the challenges of garden design is to create living paintings as seen from the fixed points of view and at the same time create an unfolding series of compellingly beautiful vignettes as we journey along the path.

Space and Light

How we experience space and light is the essence of garden design. Space is everywhere. It has no limit, and it penetrates everything. An atom is mostly space, and therefore everything made up of atoms—the trees, the rocks, the birds and lizards—are mostly space. Space has no boundary. Yet only within a boundary can we understand space. Therefore, one of the ways to influence the experience of space is to play with boundaries and the relationships among things within and outside them.

Connecting the foreground, midground, and background of a view is a technique for controlling the experience of perspective and establishing relationships among both objects and empty space. By manipulating these relationships, designers can change our experience of space in the garden.

Perhaps there is a mountain in the background. If we place a stone that has form, color, and/or texture similar to the mountain near the viewer and then place another one in the middle of the garden in such a way that the viewing corridor links the two garden rocks with the background mountain in the distance, we establish a spatial relationship in the garden. We also bring the mountain view into our direct experience by linking it to what is directly in front of us.

Foreground, midground, and background relationships also influence our sense of scale. If the foreground rock in the scene we are discussing is eight feet tall, the midground stone is four feet tall, and the mountain is what it is, the experience is quite different than if instead the foreground rock were four feet and the midground rock were eight feet, since the laws of perspective cue us to equal-sized objects getting smaller as they move away from us.

If we have a large rock in the foreground and an equal-sized one in the midground, the midground stone will appear smaller. But if we place a smaller rock in the midground, it may appear that the distance between the rocks is significantly longer. If on the other hand, the midground rock was larger than the one in the foreground, it may appear to be the same height as the foreground stone. This would foreshorten the experience of distance. This technique can be applied to any class of objects: rocks, trees, flowers, statues, lanterns, and so forth.

Another method of playing with space and boundaries, similar to the foreground/midground/background technique, is borrowed scenery. Perhaps there is a mountain in the distance that can be seen from some point in the garden. But between the mountain and the garden there might be some other object that distracts from the view of the mountain, such as a building. Placing a tree at just the right height and just the right place to hide the distraction essentially "borrows" the view of the mountain and makes it part of the garden experience.

Another means of borrowing views or objects is to imitate the borrowed form in the garden itself, so that the eye sees the object in the garden and then is naturally drawn to the object in the distance outside the garden. This links the microcosm (the garden) to the macrocosm (the world beyond its boundaries). It joins the garden mandala with the expanded mandala of the environment surrounding the garden.

We can borrow nearly anything from our surroundings: a mountain or a neighbor's tree, or perhaps a steeple or a mesa. A good design places a sitting area in just the right place and height so that the water it overlooks reflects—and borrows—the sky.

Within the boundary, space is divided by landforms, pathways, stopping places, structures, gathering places, mountains, valleys, streams, glades, and forests. Together all of these components are parts of the garden, but the garden is something much greater.

We experience space and light simultaneously. Light has physical, emotional, and psychological impacts, and it shapes our experience of space.

The designer has many ways to use light to experience the space of the garden and must explore how the structure, the water, and the plants affect the light and are affected by the light.

With trees, we can create various kinds of shade: the filtered light of an acacia or the dense shade of a linden and everything in between. Shrubs can direct views. They can be boundaries as well as forms within a boundary. For example, we may design a walk through a hedgerow, a dark corridor, which then emerges to the vista of a vast pond filled with lotus flowers, fish, and sky.

We commonly think that when we walk a pathway bordered by tall walls on both sides that we are experiencing the walls flanking us. We are actually experiencing bounded space, and how that space is illuminated changes the way we experience it.

Light penetrates living walls. We can take an experience of claustrophobia caused by a walkway enclosed by tall walls and change it to a joyful feeling of walking through a forest of gentle plants twice our size. A major factor in this experience is that the shrub wall is alive and the structural wall is not. However, how can we know that without including light?

Conscious use of space can turn a small garden into an experience of infinity. For example, a clear pond reflects the sky and duplicates all its surroundings, making the space appear larger and joining the sky to the earth. A properly trimmed tree can allow us to see its branches as well as the space beyond it, like a translucent cloth that both obscures and reveals the movements of a dancer.

SUGGESTED READING

Spirituality/Buddhism

Chödrön, Pema. *How to Meditate: A Practical Guide to Making Friends with Your Mind*. Louisville, CO: Sounds True, 2013.

Dalai Lama. *Beyond Religion: Ethics for a Whole World*. Mariner Books, 2012.

Dalai Lama and Jeffrey Hopkins. *How to Practice: The Way to a Meaningful Life*. New York: Atria Books, 2003.

Dalai Lama and Jeffrey Hopkins. *How to See Yourself as You Really Are*, reprint ed. New York: Atria Books, 2007.

Rockwell, Irini. *The Five Wisdom Energies: A Buddhist Way of Understanding Personalities, Emotions, and Relationships*. Boston: Shambhala Publications, 2002.

Shantideva. *A Guide to the Bodhisattva's Way of Life*. Dharamsala, India: Library of Tibetan Works and Archives, 1979.

Suzuki, Shunryu. *Zen Mind, Beginner's Mind*. Boston: Shambhala Publications, 2011.

Trungpa, Chögyam. *Cutting Through Spiritual Materialism*. Boston: Shambhala Publications, 2002.

Trungpa, Chögyam. *Training the Mind and Cultivating Loving-Kindness*. Boston: Shambhala Publications, 2003.

Trungpa, Chögyam. *True Perception: The Path of Dharma Art*, 2nd rev. ed. Boston: Shambhala Publications, 2008.

Landscape Architecture/Design

Cooper, David E. *A Philosophy of Gardens*. Oxford: Clarendon Press, 2006.

McHarg, Ian. *Design with Nature*, republished ed. Hoboken, NJ: John Wiley & Sons, 1995.

Mosko, Martin and Alxe Noden. *Landscape as Spirit: Creating a Contemplative Garden*. Boston: Shambhala Publications, 2003.

Treib, Marc, ed. *Meaning in Landscape Architecture and Gardens*. New York: Routledge, 2011.

Japanese Gardens

Brown, Kendall H. and David Cobb. *Quiet Beauty: The Japanese Gardens of North America*. Clarendon, VT: Tuttle Publishing, 2013.

Buck, Leslie. *Cutting Back: My Apprenticeship in the Gardens of Kyoto*. Portland, OR: Timber Press, 2017.

Keane, Marc P. *Japanese Garden Notes: A Visual Guide to Elements and Design*. Albany, CA: Stone Bridge Press, 2017.

Slawson, David A. *Secret Teachings in the Art of Japanese Gardens: Design Principles, Aesthetic Values*. New York: Kodansha International, 2013.

Takei, Jiro and Marc P. Keane. *Sakuteiki. Visions of the Japanese Garden*. Clarendon, VT: Tuttle Publishing, 2001.

Photograph by Nicholas DeSciose

ABOUT THE AUTHORS

Martin Mosko (Hakubai Daishin) is the abbot of Hakubai Temple in Boulder, Colorado, where he teaches Buddhism and design. He is a graduate of Yale University, where he studied art and Sanskrit. In 1974 he founded Marpa, a landscape architecture and building firm whose gardens have won numerous awards and have been published in magazines and books throughout the world.

Alxe Noden is a writer, filmaker, and photographer who has written several other books, including *Landscape as Spirit: Creating a Contemplative Garden* (with Martin Mosko), and has made a documentary about the creation of a contemplative garden. She has studied Tibetan Buddhism both in the United States and abroad for more than twenty-five years.

Martin and Alxe travel the country lecturing and leading workshops in contemplative garden design, photography, and meditation.